CREATED TO PRAISE

CREATED TO PRAISE

The Language of Gerard Manley Hopkins

MARGARET R. ELLSBERG

New York   Oxford
OXFORD UNIVERSITY PRESS
1987

Oxford University Press

Oxford   New York   Toronto
Delhi   Bombay   Calcutta   Madras   Karachi
Petaling Jaya   Singapore   Hong Kong   Tokyo
Nairobi   Dar es Salaam   Cape Town
Melbourne   Auckland

and associated companies in
Beirut   Berlin   Ibadan   Nicosia

Copyright © 1987 by Oxford University Press, Inc.

Published by Oxford University Press, Inc.,
200 Madison Avenue, New York, New York 10016

Oxford is a registered trademark of Oxford University Press

Library of Congress Cataloging-in-Publication Data
Ellsberg, Margaret R.
   Created to praise.
   Bibliography: p.   Includes index.
   1. Hopkins, Gerard Manley, 1844–1889—Language.
2. Theology in literature.   3. Catholic Church in literature.
4. Sacraments in literature.   I. Title.
PR4803.H44Z626   1986   821'.8   86–5194
ISBN 0-19-504098-8 (alk. paper)

10 9 8 7 6 5 4 3 2 1
Printed in the United States of America
on acid-free paper

For Robert

Acknowledgments

For expertise, affection, support of diverse kinds, and encouragement, I want to thank William Van Etten Casey, S.J., Joseph A. Devenny, S.J., George F. Schreiner, and Henry S. Woodbridge, under whose roof I wrote this book. To the teachers who first introduced me to Gerard Manley Hopkins—William Alfred, Peter Dale, and the late Robert Lowell—I express deep gratitude, for their inspiration, generosity, and brilliance. Special thanks to Clarissa Atkinson, Guy Martin, and Richard R. Niebuhr, who read this manuscript carefully and critically in its first draft.

I have used the following editions of Hopkins' works; all are reproduced by permission of Oxford University Press: W. H. Gardner and N. H. Mackenzie, eds., *The Poems of Gerard Manley Hopkins* (fourth edition, 1967); Humphry House and Graham Storey, eds., *The Journals and Papers of Gerard Manley Hopkins* (1959); C. C. Abbott, ed., *The Letters of Gerard Manley Hopkins to Robert Bridges* (1935); C. C. Abbott, ed., *The Correspondence of Gerard Manley Hopkins and Richard Watson Dixon* (1935); C. C. Abbott, ed., *Further Letters of Gerard Manley Hopkins* (1938); Christopher J. Devlin, S.J., *The Sermons and Devotional Writings of Gerard Manley Hopkins* (1959).

Contents

CREATED TO PRAISE

Introduction

Solidly established since the 1930s as a major poet, the Victorian Jesuit Gerard Manley Hopkins ironically did not write for publication and had no explicit intention of being read. Free from an obligation to write regularly or predictably, he could be wildly experimental and work totally upon inspiration. Among the first critics to applaud Hopkins' unusual work was F. R. Leavis, who claimed, "He was one of the most remarkable technical inventors who ever wrote."[1] It has remained an assumption that if Hopkins was better than other poets, it is because he was more innovative. His whole career, poetic and personal, was more, however, than innovation. It was a campaign against staleness and indistinctness. His poetry eventually became, above all, the sovereign expression of himself: his distinctive genius and religious discipline became increasingly blended with the marks and qualities of his personality. In what follows I hope to examine his achievement within the limited context that he imposed on himself—the context of an English Catholic clergyman in the two decades following the First Vatican Council, living under a vow of religious obedience, choosing daily to control his poetic talent in the interest of serv-

3

ing what to him was a higher end, and yet writing poetry throughout his life. Between the time he composed his first major poem, "The Wreck of the Deutschland," which his superior asked him to write, and the last five years of his life, when he described his poems as coming to him "unbidden and against my will," he wrote only when he felt his poetic gift to be in coincidence with, or in the service of, that higher end. He was a natural writer working against almost incredible odds. Yet, these very odds provided the forge for a process that he was to call "selving." By this Hopkins meant the phenomenon of a creature becoming its own most exact self, reflecting and returning to God its own ultimate distinctiveness. I hope to discuss here the hard process by which Hopkins both as person and poet "selved."

During his twelve years as an active poet and Jesuit, Hopkins worked relentlessly to make aesthetic and eventually theological sense of a world of apparently unrelated particulars, an effort he began by entering the Catholic Church and by choosing an exceptionally stringent discipline within the Church. He pursued this effort and this discipline in all the poems he wrote. In a process that culminates during the Long Retreat of his Tertianship in 1881, it becomes more certain and more manifest that his choice to become a Catholic was, whether consciously or not, completely coherent with a choice to become a certain kind of poet.

Hopkins' career was brief, and his poems fill one short volume. He left, however, five volumes of prose: three books of letters, a volume of sermons and devotional writing, and his notebooks. These reveal a character of philosophic tendencies, unflinching moral audacity, childlike curiosity, and devout personal affections. His prose delivers an image of a spirit that was anything but thwarted or deprived. The notebooks, dating from his boyhood, are at once scholarly and inventive, filled with detail and signs of those arresting traits that we associate with strong personality. His sermons and devotional writings give one access to his experience of Jesuit spirituality and of the thirteenth-century Franciscan Scholastic Duns Scotus, both of which profoundly affected his approach to his own poetry.

The devotional writings would be of great interest to theologians and church historians had he never written anything else; something similar can be said of his letters. His personal correspondence reconstructs a poetic system, since— like that of Keats—it contains much original literary theory. Hopkins wrote almost all of his letters to Robert Bridges (later poet laureate) and Canon Richard Watson Dixon. A volume of *Further Letters* contains his various other correspondence. Neither Bridges nor Dixon (but especially Bridges) found it easy to understand Hopkins, and many of his letters consisted of elaborate defenses and explications of his poems. These explications were invariably assertive, indisputable, and charmingly cocksure: "Some of my rhymes I regret, but they are past changing, grubs in amber: there are only a few of these; others are unassailable; some others again there are which malignity may munch at but the Muses love."[2] And in his claim that there were "excellences" in verse that were "higher" than immediate intelligibility, he could not have been more insistent. He was often trying, he said, "to express a subtle and recondite thought on a subtle and recondite subject in a subtle and recondite way, and with great felicity and perfection . . . [and] something must be sacrificed, with so trying a task, in the process."[3] These letters disclose confidence and persuasiveness, but also wit, resilience, charm, affection, and the very eccentricities that more sentimental readers have since found so lovable in Hopkins. "*Dearest* Bridges," Hopkins addresses him. Hardly breathes a modern critic who has not expressed irritation at Bridges for failing to be convinced by Hopkins' devoted efforts to convert him to his ideas of poetry. To the critical in-

troduction Bridges wrote for Hopkins' first edition, a group
of anonymous Jesuits responded. Their essay began:

> Thirty years have passed over his grave and Gerard Hop-
> kins remains the elusive Jesuit, the obscure melodist, the
> lost Victorian. Only a gossamer web cut out of his shim-
> mering life hangs in the memory of the few who remem-
> ber. Of these the remembrance of the Laureate provokes
> comment, since he seems under the delusion that Jesuitry
> ruined his poetry (as Pascal would have prophesied) and
> that Gerard caged himself in a religious prison amid the
> political Yahoos and clerics of Dublin like some bright
> plumaged songster in a bat-tenanted belfry. Otherwise it
> is difficult to understand Mr. Bridges' curious impertinence
> or vulgar obtuseness, or to excuse his idiot shudder over
> the last "terrible" and posthumous sonnets. The word
> "terrible" has become terrible only in its meaninglessness.[4]

This observation of "Mr. Bridges' curious impertinence or
vulgar obtuseness" is the characteristic, and to an extent,
understandable response to his objections.

Bridges' own letters to Hopkins are presumed destroyed—
only three are included in Bridges' published correspon-
dence.[5] But one letter to Hopkins' mother, written about a
year after her son's death, seems particularly indicting: "I
should myself prefer the postponement of the poems til a
memoir is written, *or* I have got my own method of prosody
recognised separately from Gerard's. They are the same, and
he has the greater claim than I do to the origination of it."[6]
Of this the reviewer for *Times Literary Supplement* wrote,
"It is hard to get round this: Bridges is putting his own in-
terests (the interests of his own theory of prosody) before
those of his friend, and that must—surely—be wrong."[7] Bridges
did, in fact, wait thirty years before publishing Hopkins'
poems. His "Preface" accompanying that first edition—in-
tended in his own words to "put the poems out of the reach

of criticism"[8]—so strenuously anticipated a bad reception
that the "Preface" itself became a criticism, a documenta-
tion of Bridges' own cautious, patrician decorum warning
the reader against Hopkins' unpredictable vitality. And yet,
it could be argued that, personal motives aside, Bridges was
wise to wait thirty years[9]—and should have waited forty—
since the cultural climate in 1889 (the year of Hopkins'
death) was by no means ready for this bewildering genius.
The controversy over Bridges' actions as Hopkins' quasi-
literary executor is a classic, and one much raked over. Of
importance here is the fact that Hopkins ardently cherished
this odd friendship which provided him with such a tough
audience of one. When he finally produced a volume in
1918, Bridges prefaced the edition with a dedicatory sonnet:

> Our generation already is overpast,
> And thy lov'd legacy, Gerard, hath lain
> Coy in my home; as once thy heart was fain
> Of shelter, when God's terror held thee fast
> In life's wild wood at Beauty and Sorrow aghast;
> Thy sainted sense trammel'd in ghostly pain,
> Thy rare ill-broker'd talent in disdain:
> Yet love of Christ will win man's love at last.
> Hell wars without; but, dear, the while my hands
> Gathered thy book, I heard, this wintry day,
> Thy spirit thank me, in his young delight
> Stepping again upon the yellow sands.
> Go forth: amid our chaffinch flock display
> Thy plumage of far wonder and heavenward flight![10]

Just as the correspondence with Bridges provides us with
most of Hopkins' best literary arguments, the correspon-
dence with Canon Dixon reveals reflections on his spiritual
life. Although it is probable that neither Bridges nor Dixon
fully grasped Hopkins' potential stature, the reader is privi-
leged to see Hopkins working out his theories and gaining

precision over the course of these lifelong, if largely literary, relationships.

Gerard Manley Hopkins was a character disposed to great intensity and to a stubbornness that ultimately molded itself as discipline. He was born on July 28, 1844 to wealthy High Anglican parents, the first of nine children. While he was still very young, his peculiar philosophic interests emerged: he once made his little brothers eat flowers so that they would understand what they really were.[11] He went to the Highgate School in London, where Samuel Taylor Coleridge had once taught, and there he distinguished himself as a brilliant student. At this school the Master, Mr. Dyne, treated the boys harshly at the slightest provocation, and Hopkins was often rebellious. Here Hopkins began to display the strong tendencies toward moral scrupulosity and self-discipline, almost to the point of mortification, that followed him throughout his adulthood—tendencies whose destination resides within the sonnets written in the last five years of his life.

At Highgate School Hopkins took a poetry prize, was deemed a superb scholar of Classics, and proceeded to Oxford in 1863. When he was at Oxford, he began to plan in his journals how he would take his tea in Lent and whether to abstain from pudding: his restraint, his search for personal justification and perfection, his hectoring character, all combined and found in religion a natural channel. At Oxford he abandoned contemplation of the beautiful in his poetic efforts and became scrupulous, austere, and overtly religious. During this time he wrote such poems as "Myself unholy, from myself unholy" and "The Habit of Perfection." By his second year in Oxford, what has often been isolated by scholars as the earliest sign of conflict between his poetry and religion appears in his journal: "Nov. 6. On this day by

God's grace I resolved to give up all beauty until I had His leave for it."[12] And: "No verses in Passion Week or on Fridays."[13] Also visible in the journals at this point is an increasing passion for consistency, and the obvious growth of a linguistic and literary intellect.

Many young men at Oxford were converted to Rome by the Catholicizing tendencies of the Tractarian Movement. Conversion to an absolute and dogmatic orthodoxy was probably an inevitable function of Hopkins' character, as though the historic event of the Oxford Movement coincided purely accidentally with Hopkins' choice of a Catholic life.

As the commentator, Donald McChesney, wrote:

> Hopkins wrote later in his life "that if anyone ever became a Catholic 'because two and two make four,' he did." He meant that he was intellectually convinced of the logical validity of Catholic arguments and would have gone over to Rome whatever the inward or outward obstacles. Also, there was, deep in his nature, a deep-seated hunger for absolute obedience. . . . This hunger was the obverse side of the streak of wilfulness which lay half-hidden in him; it was also his defense against the uncertainty and waywardness of his emotional nature which he described in "The Wreck of the Deutschland" as "soft sift in an hourglass."[14]

He was called "the star of Balliol" and took a Double First in Greats in 1866, but since he had decided to join the Catholic Church a few months before, against all advice and the flat commandment of his parents, his stunning academic career at Oxford was over.

Hopkins entered the Society of Jesus two years later, and at that time, presumably with a sense of dutiful humility, he burned all his poetry and entered a long period of silence.[15] He began to write again only when his superior told him to write a poem on the occasion of the sinking of the

ship *Deutschland*. The product of his obedience in this mat-
ter was "The Wreck of the Deutschland," a metrical *tour de
force* which W. H. Gardner, the editor of the fourth edition
of the poems, has called "the massive overture to this man's
too-brief opera." At this point, in early 1876, Hopkins was
spending his second of three years at St. Beuno's College in
North Wales. Natural beauty, peace, and contemplation
made these, according to his own letters, his happiest years.
The poem with which he broke his silence—powerful, unique,
bursting with controlled energy—embodied his mature mind
and talent. After that, he wrote in a letter, he felt "free to
compose," so long as his verses in no way interfered with his
parish work and other religious duties.

The next six years of his life were rich in poetic achieve-
ment though the poems he produced were not numerous.
He was frequently exhausted and suffered from physical ail-
ments. Hopkins found parish work among the poor depress-
ing, and his letters complain almost constantly of his never
having enough time for things. He defended his choices by
saying that his priestly work was "for the kingdom of heav-
en's sake." He was oppressed by an inability to finish work
that he undertook and indeed left many fragments of poems,
lectures, and commentaries. The great and conflicting ver-
satility of his talents, his feeling that in the order of things
his parish duties should come first, scholarship second, and
poetry only if time remained, and a constitutional tendency
to nervous prostrations—all of these conspired to make his
daily life one of suffering and affliction.

Yet during these Jesuit years Hopkins developed not
only his spirituality but many of the literary theories that
had begun to brew during his "long silence" and even be-
fore. The most famous examples of his inventive imagina-
tion, the terms "inscape" and "instress," had entered his vo-
cabulary the year that he became a Catholic, when he was

twenty-two. Both of these terms, of such great interest and yet so elusive of exact definition, ontologically burdened Hopkins at that time. *Inscape* was the absolute selfhood of something in harmony with other things; the more inscape something had, the more *being* it had. The more one could "take in" an inscape, or instress it, the greater one's powers of perception. "All the world is full of inscape," he wrote in his journal, "and chance left free to act falls into an order as well as purpose."[16] And later he wrote to Bridges, "As air, melody, is what strikes me most of all in music, and design in painting, so design, pattern or what I am in the habit of calling 'inscape' is what I above all aim at in poetry."[17] *Instress* is the undercurrent of energy, the inner pressure that holds things up and together and gives them observable intelligibility. One reason that these words are so difficult to define is that Hopkins himself used them in different ways on different occasions. He invented them at least partly to justify the way he saw things—simply, inscape is the form of a thing, especially as it reveals some strain of universal form or harmony; instress is the recognition or feeling of the force of an inscape. He also played with such terms as "rhyme" and "pitch" and "selving," which like inscape and instress have both literary and metaphysical implications.

In 1884 Hopkins was sent to Dublin to be a professor of classics at John Henry Newman's Catholic University. He was barely forty years old, but the image of Hopkins presented by himself and others is of a slight, overwrought priest, suffering chronically from eyestrain, headaches, anemia, and depression, hating above all the burdens of giving sermons and of teaching, grading Greek exams so scrupulously that he found himself unable, from exhaustion, to add up his own fractions. He wrote to Bridges,

I have a salary of £400 a year, but when I first contem-
plated the six examinations I have yearly to conduct, five
of them running, and to the Matriculation there came up
last year 750 candidates, I thought that Stephen's Green
(the biggest square in Europe) paved with gold would
not pay for it. It is an honour and an opening and has
many bright sides, but at present it has also some dark
ones and this in particular that I am not at all strong, not
strong enough for the requirements, and do not see at all
how I am to be so.[18]

On one occasion he was discovered at three in the morning
with his head wrapped in wet towels, sobbing over a set of
grades. During these years in Dublin the strange mixture of
brilliance and limitation produced the so-called Terrible
Sonnets. Humble obedience, so long in dangerous titration
with the arrogance of his totalitarian will, lost its equilib-
rium in this period of deep fatigue as he approached at last
and with explosive power the central questions of the spir-
itual life—aridity, the essential quality of humanity as morally
free, the bitterness of pride, the cohabitation of sin and
grace in human life.

His studies of Duns Scotus had given Hopkins' earlier
poems philosophic power; his confrontation with what might
be called original sin gives the Terrible Sonnets moral power.
Hopkins said that they were "written in blood," "unbidden
and against my will"—for it did not suit his will to write
about his most personal concern, the struggling relationship
between his will and God's. Yet in these sonnets of desola-
tion, the last poems of his life, Hopkins arrived at the con-
clusive confrontation between his vocations as priest and
poet. And although they may have been "written in blood,"
they were channelled with the same perfect metrical preci-
sion as his earlier efforts. Their greatness must be seen not
only in their technical achievement but in what they reveal,
so powerfully, about the spiritual life. This final period of

his career, while bleak, while marked by what he called "fits of sadness so severe they resemble madness," nevertheless also produced "That Nature is a Heraclitean Fire and of the comfort of the Resurrection," in which Hopkins, the "mortal trash" of sinful humanity, "in a flash" becomes "what Christ is . . . / Immortal diamond." His dying words were, "I am so happy." He died in Dublin in 1889 of typhus, at the age of forty-four.

➤ In 1976 he was established in Poet's Corner in Westminster Abbey, the highest posthumous honor that can be bestowed on an English poet. Whereas other poets in Westminster Abbey had as their epitaphs whole stanzas or groups of lines from their own work, Hopkins' stone—reflecting the compression, the extraordinary control, the rare cut and multi-faceted quality of his poems—bears only two words: "Immortal Diamond."

Hopkins has not inspired a unified body of criticism. Above all, his work has stimulated relentless controversy. Robert Bridges included a few pages of his poetry in an anthology called *The Spirit of Man* in 1916; in 1918 Bridges published the first edition of Hopkins' poems, a selection introduced by the often censorious essay that has become for Hopkins' defenders the proof that Bridges, and others like him, did not understand Hopkins' poetic genius. Bridges' famous introduction to this edition referred to the first poem of the selection, "The Wreck of the Deutschland," as "a dragon folded in the gate to forbid all entrance"; he furthermore attacked what he saw as "the naked encounter of sensualism and asceticism," and accused Hopkins of "errors of taste." Hopkins' defenders, who have been if anything more vehement and even more vituperative than his critics, too often have not noted that it was Bridges alone who kept copies of all of Hopkins' poems over the years (Hopkins

himself did not), who consistently encouraged him to con-
tinue writing, and who—despite their major differences of
temperament and taste, especially in religious matters—re-
mained a loyal and constant correspondent.

Hopkins' poems, composed decades before they were pub-
lished, were still extremely revolutionary when they were
issued in 1918, and the reactions they provoked were mixed.
In the 1920s they attracted the attention of such eminent
critics as I. A. Richards and William Empson, who liked
them very much, and Yvor Winters, who disliked them, and
Yeats (who called him a Mannerist), and Eliot (who called
him minor). Enjoyment and appreciation of Hopkins' po-
etry was then, as now, very much a question of taste. A. E.
Housman's response to Robert Bridges for a gift copy of the
Hopkins' edition made the point:

> Sprung Rhythm, as he calls it in his sober and sensible
> preface, is just as easy to write as other forms of verse; and
> many a humble scribbler of words for music-hall songs has
> written it well. But he does not: he does not make it audi-
> ble; he puts light syllables in the stress and heavy syllables
> in the slack, and has to be helped out with typographical
> signs explaining that things are to be understood as being
> what in fact they are not.[19]

It took over ten years to sell the first printing of seven hun-
dred and fifty copies.[20] With the publication of the second
edition in 1930, edited and enlarged by Charles Williams,
critical attention, including that of W. H. Auden and F. R.
Leavis, began to grow. By the centenary of Hopkins' birth,
1944, some of the most famous studies of his work were
either in print or soon to be, and these are the classics for
students of Hopkins.[21]

As his letters, journals, and devotional writings were col-
lected and published, and his reputation became more as-
sured, the volume of critical writings about Hopkins in-

creased steadily. All of his original writings have been published now, with the exception of some confessional notes that are held by the Society of Jesus at Farm Street in London. At the time of Hopkins' death in 1889, what could be found of his papers in his room in Dublin was distributed among his family, Campion Hall, and Farm Street. Some things were burnt by his request. There are well over a hundred books in print on Hopkins, including a good annotated bibliography.[22] And in each of the last twenty years the International M.L.A. Bibliography has recorded between sixty and one hundred articles written about him.

In the last decade, two new biographies of Hopkins have been published.[23] The task of writing a biography of Hopkins poses particular problems since he entered religious life at the age of twenty-four, and external events after that point were few; to document the more arresting events of his life—spiritual and poetic—would require an extensive, critical biography, which has yet to be written.[24]

This book will be divided into four chapters. In the first I will review one of the questions which has most concerned interpreters—the conflict between Hopkins' vocations as priest and poet. In the other chapters, I hope to show in three consecutive and related arguments that Hopkins' poetic language was a direct function of his religious thought.

Again and again the two vocations have been treated as incompatible, as producing a tension that was detrimental to his productivity and his health. "Humanly speaking he made a grievous mistake in joining the Jesuits," wrote C. N. Luxmoore in a letter of reminiscence to Hopkins' brother Arthur, "for on further acquaintance his whole soul must have revolted. . . . To get on with the Jesuits you must become on many grave points a machine, without will, without conscience, and that to his nature was an impossibility.

To his lasting honor be it said he was too good for them."[25]
This represents the critical extreme, which claims that reli-
gious life, and especially the rule of obedience, crippled
Hopkins' ego and broke his genius. There is an opposite ex-
treme, usually occupied by Roman Catholic critics, which
celebrates how religion and the Society of Jesus formed and
more or less effortlessly assured his poetic genius. An anony-
mous Jesuit contemporary described Hopkins in a way that,
as it turned out, fell somewhere between these two extremes:

> What struck me most of all in him was his child-like guile-
> lessness and simplicity. . . . Joined to this and closely
> connected with it, was his purity of heart. . . . He had a
> distinct dash of genius. His opinion on any subject in
> Heaven and earth was always fresh and original. . . . He
> was also most sensitive and this caused him to suffer much.
> I have rarely known anyone who sacrificed so much in
> taking the yoke of religion. If I had known him outside
> [of the Jesuits], I should have said that his love of specu-
> lation and originality of thought would make it almost im-
> possible for him to submit his intellect to authority.[26]

Hopkins himself explicitly expressed his experience of two
vocations, and it is elucidated in his correspondence with
Dixon.[27] Beyond what Hopkins himself has revealed, it may
be inferred that the mood of praise and celebration of the
created world which poetry, especially Hopkins' poetry, re-
quires is one that Hopkins had gradually to allow himself.
As one Jesuit scholar has recently pointed out, "In Hopkins
there is no Miltonic sense that poetry can justify God's ways
to man; it is rather a private and occasional activity, to
which he sits extremely lightly. In no sense is it a part of his
apostolate, a means of fulfilling what he saw as his voca-
tion."[28] The radical asceticism that was part of the Victorian,
Anglo-Catholic movement, and of the general spirit of the
Roman Catholic Church of Vatican I, agreed well with Hop-

kins' own inclinations to austerity. As his religious faith became more incarnational and sacramental under thc influence of an Ignatian education, he increasingly sensed and expressed God's presence—first in created nature, and ultimately even in human nature. Thus, the pious, idealistic, and rhetorically brittle poems he wrote before entering the priesthood are replaced—after "The Wreck of the Deutschland"—first by celebratory, sacramental nature poems in the quasi-Romantic tradition, and ultimately by poems which try to deal with the presence of God not only in nature but in the poet's own soul.

The second chapter is about how Hopkins used sacramental language. Samuel Taylor Coleridge was another nineteenth-century poet who saw poetry as a means of communicating spiritual truth. Yet, how differently a poem by Coleridge and a poem by Hopkins on similar subjects ("Frost at Midnight" and "The Starlight Night") achieve this end will be shown by comparing their two views of sacramental belief and how that relates to their theories of language. To be part of the created world, the world of objective fact, and to be in sacramental union with God is a condition which eludes language. To insist that any natural phenomenon, including bread and wine, is actually in some absolute sense the same as God, requires a suspension of the usual logical and epistemological categories. Both Hopkins and Coleridge considered poetic language capable of enacting this suspension, though for different reasons. A belief in transubstantiation informed Hopkins' view of nature and the language he chose to describe it. For Coleridge, the subjective imagination was the transcendent force which infused natural detail with spiritual significance.

The third chapter is about what I shall call Hopkins' theology of the particular. Hopkins' epistemology is often identified with Duns Scotus' concept of *haecceitas*, or *thisness;* that is, Hopkins perceives in things their essential being, manifest in their particular incarnation. Hopkins was aware of Darwin's theory of the origin and method of classification of species, and it seems likely that this awareness would have entered Hopkins' own consciousness of the isolation and status of individual things. Hopkins' interest in the particularity of creatures begins with his recognition of the Incarnation as the central Christian principle. The intuitive relationship between particulars and God, the infinite individuality of *haecceitas,* is the Scotist version of the broader question of the relationship of individuals to universals. How Hopkins demonstrates this preoccupation in his poetry is the substance of my third chapter, in which I hope to show that the different terminologies of priest and poet become compatible through Hopkins' understanding of both the sacrament and Scotus.

The fourth chapter is an investigation of Hopkins as a poet of the Christian baroque. It will include a brief review of the baroque principle in poetry and in Jesuit spirituality, and of how Hopkins' lyrical language might be so labelled. Since the early 1970s, the number of books and articles on Hopkins' language have proliferated, and some have emphasized structuralist or purely linguistic principles in analyzing Hopkins' poetic system. The structuralist or semiotic approaches to reading literature have elicited enormous controversy, especially since they tend to trivialize language or treat it as a sort of word-puzzle. And many "new critical" campaigns have tried to dismiss biographical, historical, psychological, or spiritual aspects of a writer's achievement. Yet is this sort of "purity" ever really possible, especially with a writer like Hopkins whose language is so entangled with his deepest metaphysical involvements? Still, some of these analyses have been helpful in preparing the fourth chapter, where I attempt to establish a transhistorical or suprahistorical category for poetic language—namely, *ba-*

roque—which is usually associated with the seventeenth cen-
tury and with particular cultures and genres of art.[29]

Unlike what a "structuralist" might conclude from a read-
ing of Hopkins' poetry, I hope to prove that Hopkins' use of
language cannot be separated from the experiences, objects,
and ideas that it exists to tell of.[30] His language is both
sacramental and particular, and this combination not only
produces a baroque style—unique and elusive of category—
but reflects as well a metaphysical attitude that can also be
called baroque.

CHAPTER ONE

"Incompatible Excellences":
Hopkins' Two Vocations

Scholars and critics have taken great interest in the diffi- culty of Hopkins' language, and in the conflict between his vocations as priest and poet. Catholic readers have tended to applaud Hopkins' heroism and sanctity by emphasizing his priesthood more than his artistic gifts. Non-Catholic readers, should they be tempted to find fault, have tended to see this emphasis on his priesthood as tragic or at least psychically damaging. When Hopkins is allowed to speak for himself on this topic, there is no euphoric resolution of the conflict: he himself senses tragic waste in his life, and yet he insists that his choices reflect God's will.

W. H. Gardner adopted the terms "character" and "per- sonality" "as convenient symbols to indicate a natural di- chotomy of being which in Hopkins was particularly marked —two strains in the man which *tend* to pull in opposite di- rections."[1] "Character" he defined as "the stamp imposed upon the individual by tradition and moral training; it may also be desired and self-imposed, and in any case it is main- tained by an effort of the will."[2] Personality is the assortment of free, native tendencies that find their expression, at best, "in great works of art." In Hopkins, character was constantly under the control of the individual will, and personality was submitted to the restraining force of character. In someone of such highly determined personality as Hopkins, these acts of will and restraint were extraordinary, and his exhaustion expressed itself in physical debilitation and mental depression. "Never," said a Dublin contemporary, "was a squarer man in a rounder hole."[3] Yet, what in the unfettered personality would have been rebellion and stubbornness, in the carefully monitored and awesomely intelligent character of Hopkins became creativity and discipline. Within the context of nineteenth-century poetic religion and romantic religiosity, both poetry and religion became tightly ordered by the formal choices Hopkins made.

Although Hopkins kept no records or copies of his own work, he did write for Robert Bridges in 1883 an essay about his own poetry, briskly explaining sprung rhythm and other prosodic theories. This essay was eventually published as the "Author's Preface" in the second edition (1930) of the poems. Hopkins also told Bridges that he wanted his poems somewhere where they could be published, if someone wished, after his death. In 1887 he wrote to Canon Dixon:

> What becomes of my verses I care little, but about things like this, what I write or could write on philosophical matters, I do; and the reason of the difference is that the verses stand or fall by their simple selves and, though by being read they might do good, by being unread they do no harm; but if the other things are unsaid right they will be said by somebody else wrong, and that is what will not let me rest.[4]

It is clear that Hopkins did not deny his nature, nor reject any ambition to pursue excellence. His asceticism was simply molded, formed by Catholic and specifically Jesuit discipline. *The Spiritual Exercises,* Ignatius Loyola's handbook for members of the Society of Jesus, instructs Jesuits to seek, above all, selfless detachment and a character disciplined by meditation. "Election" or choice is required, first to choose a state of life in view of God and salvation, and then to order each detail of daily conduct according to that primary choice. St. Ignatius also designed a series of meditations on certain ideas and methods for contemplating scenes from the life of Christ. The Ignatian meditation or contemplation has been called "potential poetry,"[5] and in fact it is easy to see how the intensely directed thought of an Ignatian meditation could influence the poetic imagination:

110. THE SECOND CONTEMPLATION
  The Nativity
PRAYER. The usual preparatory prayer.

111. FIRST PRELUDE. This is the history of the mystery. Here it will be that Our Lady, about nine months with child, and, as may be piously believed, seated on an ass, set out from Nazareth. She was accompanied by Joseph and a maid, who was leading an ox. They are going to Bethlehem to pay the tribute that Caesar imposed on those lands.

112. SECOND PRELUDE. This is a mental representation of the place. It will consist here in seeing in imagination the way from Nazareth to Bethlehem. Consider its length, its breadth; whether level, or through valleys and over hills. Observe also the place or cave where Christ is born; whether big or little; whether high or low; and how it is arranged.

113. THIRD PRELUDE. This will be the same as in the preceding contemplation and identical in form with it.

114. FIRST POINT. This will consist in seeing the persons, namely, Our Lady, St. Joseph, the maid, and the Child Jesus after His birth. I will make myself a poor little un-

worthy slave, and as though present, look upon them, contemplate them, and serve them in their needs with all possible homage and deference.

Then I will reflect on myself that I may reap some fruit.

115. SECOND POINT. This is to consider, observe, and contemplate what the persons are saying, and then to reflect on myself and draw some fruit from it.

116. THIRD POINT. This will be to see and consider what they are doing, for example, making the journey and laboring that Our Lord might be born in extreme poverty, and that after many labors, after hunger, thirst, heat, and cold, after insults and outrages, He might die on the cross, and all this for me.

Then I will reflect and draw some spiritual fruit from what I have seen.

117. COLLOQUY. Close with a colloquy as in the preceding contemplation, and with the *Our Father*.[6]

The *Exercises* were to be performed for a month, or four "weeks": the first is purgative, being devoted to meditations on sin and hell; the second is devoted to "contemplations" on the life of Christ; the third is devoted to Passion Week; the fourth to the Resurrection and Ascension. The exercises are performed five times a day, for one hour each time, with much preparation and examination before and after. The experience of such a month is extremely intense, visually and emotionally vivid, mentally strenuous, and spiritually powerful. As one critic claimed, "In short, what Baudelaire and Verlaine accomplished by vice and squalor, Hopkins accomplished by being a priest."[7]

One result of this peculiar discipline when combined with Hopkins' peculiar talent was that he would never be satisfied with form taken alone. He complained of the emptiness of Swinburne's "perpetual functioning of genius without truth, feeling, or any adequate matter to be at function on,"[8] and said that Swinburne had taught us the negative lesson that "words only are only words." Of Wordsworth he said that "spiritual insight into nature" was insufficient to make his poetry great, and this was obvious because Wordsworth too often wrote with uninspired poetic diction.[9] In Hopkins it is this wholeness, this sacramental interpenetration of accidents and substance, that eventually saved him from erring on the side of either matter or spirit. In Hopkins, intensity of rhetoric and intensity of spiritual insight combine to produce one of the most complex, difficult collections of verse in the English language.

Scholars have assiduously pursued Hopkins' semantics, philology, metrics, the methods and theology of St. Ignatius, the epistemological theories of Duns Scotus, and anything else that might elucidate Hopkins' enigmatic achievement. But while all of these elements entered into his poetic processes of conception and composition, they are secondary to the profound sense of accuracy and exactitude that Hopkins brought to his writing and that he expected from his readers. This sense of accuracy took form in three tendencies in Hopkins' verse—in sacramental localization, in particularity, and in the effort to render strikingly exact the relationship between the spiritual and the material. As one of Hopkins' early defenders said, "It is in place at this point to observe that Hopkins' genius was as much a matter of rare character, intelligence, and sincerity as of technical skill: indeed, in his great poetry the distinction disappears; the technical triumph is a triumph of spirit."[10]

Hopkins' own discussion of his artistic "methods" is less helpful and ultimately less important than his advice, "Pay attention,"[11] by which he meant, read this poetry with the capacity to listen carefully, with the most receptive intelligence. And this intelligence must receive the various rhymes, resonances, and particular meanings that make difficulty an essential component of Hopkins' poetry. "It must be read *adagio molto,*" he wrote to Bridges.[12] Even read this way, however, and with the wits of the most attentive scholars, his poetry notoriously eludes definitive interpretation or exegesis. There is no simple logical or analogical poetic structure. He wrote no villanelles or sestinas. In the words of F. R. Leavis, "Hopkins is really difficult, and the difficulty is essential. If we could deceive ourselves into believing that we were reading easily his purpose would be defeated; for every word in one of his important poems is doing a great deal more work than almost any word in a poem of Robert Bridges."[13] He developed an idiosyncratic artistic *ascesis* whereby each new subject was approached with originality, without reference to previous canons set even in his own work. He apologized for his meager production: "Then again I have of myself made verse so laborious."[14]

Hopkins argued that his poetry was oral—"My verse is less to be read than heard, as I have told you before; it is oratorical"[15]—but it is oral principally in the sense of being rhetorically and rhythmically formal. It would be difficult to understand the *meaning* of one of Hopkins' poems at first hearing. Some aspects of his poetry are speech-like as well: sprung rhythm itself is the rhythm of speech ("Lashed rod"); some whole lines are more like conversation than like highly wrought verse ("Felix Randal the farrier, is he dead then?"); and some sequences of lines imitate human speech ("But how shall I . . . make me room there: / Reach me a . . . Fancy, come faster—"). He occasionally used words for their abstract, musical quality, though almost without exception, his rhetoric was chosen to function on more than one level—semantic, musical, oratorical. In fact he felt that English rhetoric needed reviving ever since Spenser had introduced "Parnassian" style. While agreeing with the artistic theories of Whitman, which claimed to avoid "poetical" diction in favor of the idioms and rhythms of common speech, Hopkins' own poetic diction was more likely to include these but also to draw on Greek canons of meter.

Hopkins devised sprung rhythm, he said, "because it is the nearest to the rhythm of prose, that is the native and natural rhythm of speech, the least forced, the most rhetorical and emphatic of all possible rhythms, combining, as it seems to me, opposite and, one would have thought, incompatible excellences, markedness of rhythm—that is rhythm's self—and naturalness of expression."[16] It is true that when English speech does not assume the rhythm of a fairly regular *iamb*, it is probably best described as having "sprung rhythm." Much English poetry had been written in so-called sprung or irregularly stressed rhythm, including much of Shakespeare and Milton, as well as the nineteenth-century poets ("No, no, go not to Lethe" or "Break, break, break, on thy cold grey stones / O sea" or "In the bald street breaks the blank day"). To mention this precedent, however, in no way reduces the surprise of such lines as "The thunder-purple seabeach plumèd purple-of-thunder" or "But ah, but o thou terrible, why wouldst thou rude on me / Thy wring-world right foot rock?" His knowledge of poetry and his excitement in possessing the language were subjected to the same controls, but also to the same release that he found in the spiritual life. Religious commitment and poetic discipline eventually became his complementary faculties, though they never merged.

In an early letter to his college friend, Urquhart, Hopkins described his religious conversion: "When it came it was all in a minute."[17] Later, and more than once, he described his poetic inspiration similarly, as being "unbidden and against my will." Although Hopkins' letters do not offer irrefragable proof that his poetry could be in a state of consolation with his religious life until the period of his Tertianship in 1881, we have much earlier indications that his spiritual and creative efforts intersect deliberately. And it was a lifelong effort to bring the two vocabularies into consonance. The first ten stanzas of his first mature poem, "The Wreck of the Deutschland," concern the historic event of the foundering of a ship off the coast of England, but also the symbolic event of material disaster and spiritual victory. These stanzas also draw on personal experiences similar to those evoked at the end of his career in the so-called Terrible Sonnets. "I may add for your greater interest and edification," he wrote to Bridges, "that what refers to myself in this poem ["Wreck"] is all strictly and literally true and did all occur; nothing is added for poetical padding."[18] A great deal of the poem refers to the poet himself. For example: "Thou mastering me / God!"; "I did say yes / O at lightning and lashed rod"; "The frown of his face / Before me, the hurtle of hell / Behind"; "I am soft sift / In an hourglass"; "Ah, touched in your bower of bone, / Are you! turned for an exquisite smart, / Have you! make words break from me here all alone / Do you!— mother of being in me, heart." These are not the words of a creature at docile ease with the image of God as a tender shepherd.

The poem begins in a rapture of tension and adoration of a masterful Lord, who gives and who takes away. "The mystery must be instressed": the innocent victims were tried and then snatched from life by the Lord of storms, "he in three of the thunder throne." This awful event must be seen as a mystery, and it must be taken in and felt as stress along every nerve and fiber. For Hopkins, "the God who is, is terrible."[19] The content of his poetic narrative reveals struggle, and the *form* implies struggle—an intensive experimentation, a fast-paced trial and probe of meters, rhymes, phonetics: "We lash with the best or worst / Word last! How a lush-kept plush-capped sloe / Will, mouthed to flesh-burst, / Gush!— flush. . . ." His search for the ideal in the particular, for the beautiful in the presence of God, for divine love in the experience of suffering, "lightning of fire hard-hurled," demanded a constant reconciliation of struggle. And ultimately, human language is inadequate to describe, define, or embody the experience of God. As J. Hillis Miller put it, "There is no word for the Word."

> "The Wreck of the Deutschland," like all the great poems of Hopkins' maturity, turns on a recognition of the ultimate failure of poetic language. Its failure is never to be able to express the inconceivable and unsayable mystery of how something that is as unique as a single word—that is, a created soul—may be transformed into the one Word, Christ, which is its model, without ceasing to be a unique and individual self.
>
> Rather than being in happy correspondence, Hopkins' theological thought and its linguistic underthought are at cross-purposes. They have a structure of chiasmus.[20]

There must also have been in Hopkins a conflict between religious silence and "self-expression" that could have been resolved only if what Hopkins "expressed" in poetry was other than "self" as ego. Annihilation of the self is never a Christian ideal; it is a Christian ideal to develop the self into a unique instrument of God's glory, the phenomenon which Hopkins labels "selving." His earlier letters to Dixon reveal this distinction:

> Then what a genius was Campion himself: was not he a poet? perhaps a great one, if he had chosen. . . . It seems in time he might have done anything. But his eloquence died on the air, his genius was quenched in his blood after one year's employment in his country.[21]

And again:

> Above all Christ our Lord: his career was cut short and, whereas he would have wished to succeed by success—for

it is insane to lay yourself out for failure, prudence is the first of the cardinal virtues, and he was the most prudent of men—nevertheless he was doomed to succeed by failure; his plans were baffled, his hopes dashed, and his work was done by being broken off undone. However much he understood all this he found it an intolerable grief to submit to it. He left an example: it is very strengthening, but except in that sense it is not consoling.[22]

It is plausible that Hopkins' confidence in his own genius was reduced partly by the cool response Bridges made to his novel techniques, and this may have raised questions in Hopkins' mind about the compatibility of poetic effort and religious perfection. His letters to Canon Dixon are probably the most revealing of Hopkins' own thoughts about his vocations. His tone in this correspondence is that of one preaching to the converted, or rather of one sharing an understood experience, since Dixon seemed to agree with Hopkins about the appropriateness of religious life. These letters of Hopkins provide the most candid and often emotional expressions of his experience of spirituality and of how he came to regard "genius" and "success" in its light. It seems that the conflict is not between abstract obedience and abstract genius, but between the particular Jesuit ministry that Hopkins had undertaken and his own wild and energetic genius.

His correspondence with Robert Bridges, while more copious, is more adversarial.[23] Bridges forced Hopkins to defend his poetry, and as a result, these letters contain Hopkins' best discussions of literary theory and of his own techniques. The letters often bear tones of irritation, exasperation, even contempt—but simultaneously of patience, loyalty, and fervor. About a year before his death he wrote to Bridges, "And there it is, I understand these things so much better than you: we should explain things, plainly state them . . . but I have the passion for explanation and you have not."[24] To

Bridges, however, the explanations are almost always literary and rarely religious; he grasps Bridges' hostility (not unusual in rational Victorian Englishmen) to Jesuit discipline, and he does not venture to confess the same struggles to him as he does to Canon Dixon. When he sent Bridges "The Wreck of the Deutschland," he explained, "I do not write for the public; you are my public and I hope to convert you."[25] Presumably he meant to convert him to his literary theories, though already these were inseparable from his Catholicism. By the time Hopkins wrote "The Wreck," his first major poem as a Jesuit, it was clear to him that no art or poetry would be for him merely aesthetic exercise.

The first sentence of the *Spiritual Exercises*—*Homo creatus est laudare*—is displayed in Hopkins himself, in his habitual or perhaps instinctive search for instress, harmony, and pattern that made artistic form an homage to the author of all form. Of this sentence Humphry House, the early editor of Hopkins' notebooks, wrote,

> No single sentence better explains the motives and direction of Hopkins' life than this, "man is created to praise." He believed it as wholly as a man can believe anything; and when regret or sorrow over anything in his life comes to a critic's mind, this must be remembered.[26]

Hopkins wrote to Bridges,

> An article by G. W. G(osse) in July's *Cornhill*, "a Plea for Certain Exotic Forms of Verse," speaks of and quotes you—a Triolet from your early book. It seems that triolets and rondels and rondeaus and chants royal and what not and anything but serving God are all the fashion.[27]

Occasionally Hopkins chastised Bridges' disapprobation sarcastically:

My dearest Bridges,—I see I must send a line to "put you
out of your agony." Want of convenience of writing was
the only cause of my delay, having both work here to do
and serious letters to write I shrank from the "distressing
subject" of rhythm on which I knew I must enter. I could
not even promise to write often or answer promptly, our
correspondence lying upon unprofessional matter. How-
ever you shall hear me soon.[28]

He contrasts the "unprofessional matter" of poetry with the
"serious letters" he has to write on the matters of his profes-
sion, that is, the priesthood. This is almost certainly an as-
sertion for Bridges' benefit, who has shown himself unsym-
pathetic or invincibly ignorant regarding Hopkins' "sacrifice."
It is easy to imagine what Bridges might have written to
elicit *this* response:

Dearest Bridges,—Your letter cannot amuse Father Provin-
cial, for he is on the unfathering deeps outward bound to
Jamaica: I shd not think of telling you anything about his
reverence's goings and comings if it were it (thus in MS.)
not that I know this fact has been chronicled in the Catho-
lic papers.[29]

In his letters to both Bridges and Dixon, one is struck by
how successfully Hopkins avoids any trace of sentimental or
pious language. The synthesis of aesthetics and philosophy,
combined with strong feeling, produces in Hopkins a tone of
wise audacity. When he did feel a contradiction between his
two vocations, or rather between his will to be a priest and
his impulse to write poetry, he wrote of it with declamatory
insistence in his letters to Dixon. "Brilliancy does not suit
us," he wrote, "genius attracts fame, and individual fame St.
Ignatius looked on as the most dangerous and dazzling of all
attractions."[30] He did add later, "Since as Solomon says,
there is a time for everything, there is nothing that does not

some day come to be, it may be that the time will come for my verses."[31]

Father Devlin, who edited Hopkins' *Sermons and Devotional Writings,* said,

> A wave of diffidence amounting almost to despair seeped up in Hopkins. It was borne in upon him that he must look on his poetic genius as an amiable weakness which a hardworking Jesuit might indulge for an hour or two occasionally. And he grasped, half-consciously but once and for all, that the secret wildness of his inspiration could never be channelled in that manner.[32]

That "wildness," of personality, brought continuously into subjection by his will, was tamed partly by the stern Jesuit discipline and partly by the astonishingly rigorous form that he chose for his poetry. It is true that Hopkins received little encouragement in his day from the Society of Jesus to pursue his idiosyncratic talent; and those who, like Bridges, had no special sympathy for Catholic discipline were likely to blame the difficulty and demands of Jesuit life for Hopkins' frequent fits of desolation and exhaustion, and for his meager poetic production. The Jesuit ideal can be described as "the pursuit of the glory of God through the salvation of others."[33] And in pursuing this ideal, a Jesuit may experience what Ignatius calls consolation—awareness of God's presence—or, if his actions are not furthering his vocation, he may experience desolation. That Hopkins frequently experienced desolation, for whatever reason, is amply documented. That his priestly duties absorbed time and energy that Hopkins could have devoted to writing is beyond doubt, but whether this is entirely to be regretted, or whether Hopkins, by avoiding the priesthood, could have escaped from a nature apparently predisposed to agonizing deliberations and scrupulosity is less certain. Humphry House wrote:

"Only what word / Wisest my heart breeds dark heaven's baffling ban / Bars of hell's spell thwarts" was not written by a man whose life was a denial of his nature, but by one whose nature in whatever life would have turned a great part of his experience into a cause of pain.[34]

Hopkins himself seems to support this supposition:

The melancholy I have all my life been subject to has become of late years not indeed more intense in its fits but rather more distributed, constant and crippling. . . . I see no ground for thinking I shall ever get over it. . . .[35]

Hopkins' imaginative and emotional expressions—his longing, yearning, suffering, incompleteness—were always governed by a choice regarding the role they would play in his religious life. He wrote to Bridges, "I saw they [poems] would not interfere with my state and vocation,"[36] and later, "I cannot in conscience spend time on poetry. . . . If someone in authority knew of my having some poems printable and suggested my doing it, I shd. not refuse, I shd. be partly, though not altogether, glad."[37] To Dixon he wrote, "My rector . . . said that he wished someone would write a poem on the subject [of the Deutschland]" and "after writing [that poem] I held myself free to compose but cannot find it in my conscience to spend time upon it."[38]As these letters imply, Hopkins maintained a *forced* inner repose throughout his life. So insofar as his personal expressions (whether poetic or philosophic) did not diverge from his intuition, the judgment of his superiors, and the Ignatian *magis*, he could pursue them. The inner repose was forced on him by an act of his own will; and as he willed to imitate Christ's act of submission, obedience offered Hopkins greater assurance of being virtuous than artistic success ever could. Christ, after all,

emptied or exhausted himself so far as that was possible,
of godhead and behaved only as God's slave, as his crea-
ture, as man, which also he was. . . . It was this holding
of himself back, and not snatching at the truest and high-
est good that was his right, nay his possession . . . which
seems to me the root of all his holiness and the imitation of
this the root of all moral good in other men.[39]

The imitation of Christ's emptying, his exhaustion, and his
"holding of himself back" was to Hopkins "the root of all
moral good in other men."

Recognizing that moral goodness was Hopkins' ideal, I
would argue that he possessed more equanimity regarding
his suffering in the service of God than most of his observers
have supposed. Sometimes he served through art even though
there is clearly a struggle and a sense of contradiction be-
tween the character of self-denial and the personality of
self-expression. Consider his sonnet "Felix Randal," a poem
about the common, homely, priestly tasks of attending the
sick and anointing the dying. In describing having sat at the
bedside of Felix and having comforted him, Hopkins turns
the overwhelming natural fact of this blacksmith into a *me-
mento mori* in sprung rhythm:

> How far from then forethought of, all thy more boisterous
>   years,
> When thou at the random grim forge, powerful amidst peers,
> Didst fettle for the great grey drayhorse his bright and
>   battering sandal!

This poem, so full of Hopkins' personality, does not pretend
to reimagine the personality of Felix; it grasps his physical
"inscape," but this of course would be of interest primarily
to Hopkins as the perceiver. As Philip Endean, S.J., has de-
scribed it,

The subject matter of this poem clearly derives from his work in the slums of Lancashire; the writing is inescapably that of the Star of Balliol. Its power lies in the pathos of the incongruity between the nervous, bookish curate and the brawny blacksmith, and is inseparable from the failure actually to achieve an idiom in which the priest could relate to Felix. The poem is, of course, a private reflection on priestly work, and as such at a remove from it; what it is not, nor ever could be, is priestly work itself.[40]

What Hopkins achieves during this period is not some sense that to be a priest and to be a poet—especially the sort of poet he was—are the same thing, but rather, an increasingly sacramental sense of God's presence in nature. This sense, which will be discussed in the next chapter, gradually and incrementally gave Hopkins a particular poetic voice that he would never have found without the special education that the priesthood gave him. Humphry House isolated a "crisis of election" that Hopkins must have undergone in November 1881, during the Thirty-Day Retreat of his Tertianship. Hopkins' correspondence with Canon Dixon documents this crisis, wherein Hopkins apparently meditated on whether or not his writing poetry was pleasing to God. The letters to Dixon, written between October 10, 1881 and August 1882, describe his process of election. Election or choice is the essential spiritual movement of the *Spiritual Exercises*, which are followed for thirty days during the Tertianship (the thirteenth year) of a Jesuit's career. St. Ignatius devotes some pages of the *Exercises* to instructing the exercitant in ways of making "a good and correct choice of a way of life":

179. SECOND POINT. It is necessary to keep as my aim the end for which I am created, that is, the praise of God our Lord and the salvation of my soul. Besides this, I must be indifferent, without any inordinate attachment, so that

I am not more inclined or disposed to accept the object in question than to relinquish it, nor to give it up than to accept it. I should be like a balance at equilibrium, without leaning to either side, that I might be ready to follow whatever I perceive is more for the glory and praise of God our Lord and for the salvation of my soul.

180. THIRD POINT. I should beg God our Lord to deign to move my will, and to bring to my mind what I ought to do in this matter that would be more for His praise and glory. Then I should use the understanding to weigh the matter with care and fidelity, and make my choice in conformity with what would be more pleasing to His most holy will.[41]

After his retreat and having meditated upon the choice of a way of life according to the *Exercises*, Hopkins' letters to Dixon imply that he is in a state of "consolation" (Ignatius' term) regarding his two vocations. Especially important was the letter written on the feast of Edmund Campion, December 1, 1881, in response to the discussion that he and Dixon had been carrying on for several letters. On November 2 Hopkins had written:

This I say: my vocation puts before me a standard so high that a higher can be found nowhere else. The question then for me is whether I am willing (if I may guess what is in your mind) to make a sacrifice of hopes of fame (let us suppose), but whether I am not to undergo a severe judgment from God for the lothness I have shewn in making it, for the reserves I may have in my heart made, for the backward glances I have given with my hand upon the plough, for the waste of time the very compositions you admire may have caused and their preoccupation of the mind which belonged to more sacred or more binding duties. . . .[42]

Two days later Dixon replied:

MY DEAR, DEAR FRIEND,—Your letter touches & moves me more than I can say. I ought not in your present circumstances tease you with the regret that much of it gives me: to hear of your having destroyed poems, & feeling that you have a vocation in comparison of which poetry & the fame that might assuredly be yours is nothing. I could say much, for my heart bleeds: but I ought also to feel the same: and do not as I ought, though I thought myself very indifferent as to fame. So I will say nothing, but cling to the hope that you will find it consistent with all & that in so doing you may be sanctioned & encouraged by the great Society to which you belong, which has given so many ornaments to literature. Surely one vocation cannot destroy another: and such a Society as yours will not remain ignorant that you have such gifts as have seldom been given by God to man.[43]

On December 1, as soon as he came out of his Thirty-Day Retreat, Hopkins responded with an important statement of position about his two vocations:

Now if you value what I write, if I do myself, much more does our Lord. And if he chooses to avail himself of what I leave at his disposal he can do so with a felicity and with a success which I could never command. And if he does not, then two things follow; one that the reward I shall nevertheless receive from him will be all the greater; the other that then I shall know how much a thing contrary to his will and even to my own best interests I should have done if I had taken things into my own hands and forced on publication. This is my principle and this in the main has been my practice . . . to live by faith . . . is very hard; nevertheless by God's help I shall always do so.

Our Society values, as you say, and has contributed to literature, to culture; but only as a means to an end. Its history and its experience shew that literature proper, as poetry, has seldom been found to be to that end a very serviceable means.[44]

Neither of the extreme arguments about Hopkins' two vocations—that the priesthood completed and glorified his talent, or that it nearly killed it—confronts the undeniable fact that Hopkins chose, continually, both of them. Their coexistence was the essential expression of his very self, his nature, his inscape.

He wrote to Bridges that poetry was "unprofessional"; he wrote to Dixon that "my vocation puts before me a standard so high that a higher can be found nowhere else,"[45] and that he left the use of his talent entirely at God's "disposal." Quite probably the religious perfection that Hopkins sought in the strictness of the Jesuit ideal and the poetic perfection he found in his extraordinary metrical feats united in a new way in the last poems of his life—giving way to a moral power and honesty that added a mature intelligence to the flash and dazzle of the earlier poems. These Terrible Sonnets addressed the most intimate and compelling problems of spiritual life:

> His scholar's mind had long since formed a habit of poetic expression which channeled even these most passionate works into an elaborately ruled form, whence they derive much of their beauty. Hopkins' greatness of spirit charges their beauty with power; they testify to a great victory over pride and punctilio. Mere dogged duty won the battle, and its weapons were exhaustion, dryness, desolation, and, finally, faith.[46]

These sonnets also reveal Hopkins' loneliness, which in his case was an isolation of mind and spirit as much as a condition of solitude. He had written to Bridges, "You give me a long jobation about eccentricities. Alas, I have heard so much about and suffered so much for and in fact been so completely ruined for life by my alleged singularities that they are a sore subject."[47] Indeed, almost every peculiarity reported by biographers of Hopkins has dwelled on his wilfulness and scrupulosity. He went without liquid for twenty-one days when he was a schoolboy; he insisted against ponderous objections on becoming a Roman Catholic; he sought within the Jesuits an exactitude and rigor of observance that caused his superiors to bid him cease; he insisted on reviewing the use of his poetic talent to check constantly its suitability to religious life; his fastidiousness about grading examinations was notorious; he punished his verse to make every line rhetorically and metrically perfect. St. Ignatius himself cautions against scrupulosity, asserting that "we must put aside all judgment of our own."[48] And he continues in this vein:

> If a devout soul wishes to do something that is not contrary to the spirit of the Church or the mind of superiors and that may be for the glory of God our Lord, there may come a thought or temptation from without not to say or do it. [This may be] motivated by vainglory or some other imperfect intention, etc.[49]

Scruples and neurotic guilt can become sinful because they are designed and controlled by the human will instead of by God's will. Weary to the point of illness, Hopkins in Dublin seemed able to scruple no more, and though eventually he would complain, "Sweet fire the sire of muse, my soul needs this; / I want the one rapture of an inspiration" ("To R.B."), he was able to bring forth the eight Terrible Sonnets. These last poems differ from his earlier ones: their authentic voice echoes the voice of his letters; they are spare self-revelations. There is no distance, no elaborate indirectness of speech. They address God without formality ("O thou my friend") and cry out for help and comfort. For the first time in his life, Hopkins asks for mercy, and he asks it of God. In their intense relation to God, these poems escape the sin of despair—though they are also justly called the "sonnets of desolation."

St. Ignatius describes desolation as a predictable part of the spiritual journey, as "darkness of soul, turmoil of spirit, inclination to what is low and earthly, restlessness rising from many disturbances and temptations which lead to want of faith, want of hope, want of love."[50] That Hopkins is able in these sonnets to detail those *wants* reveals a new poetic expression not only of his relationship to God, but of his awareness of himself, of his own nature and status as a dependent creature, morally free yet needy:

> In Hopkins' terms, only through Christ can a man selve. Man selves ("the just man justices") through the exercise of his moral free will, by sin and the practice of virtue. Hopkins called Lucifer's sin, "instressing his own inscape," choosing to form and enjoy his own will apart from God's. That sin is Pride, the first and deadliest of the Deadly Sins. Hopkins knew that he had not completely formed his will in union with the will of God.[51]

The Terrible Sonnets express not despair, and not even total desolation, but rather, self-revulsion, yearning, and need. Significantly, Hopkins as the priest is using poetry as the medium of his most powerful prayer.

Hopkins said that many of these sonnets had come to him "unbidden and against my will." As he ceased to *try* to separate his ascetic morality from his poetic impulses, his poetry became flooded with the moral insight that twenty years of conscientious study of the *Spiritual Exercises* and self-examination had given him. In these poems his usual consciousness of nature, his intelligence about poetry, and his theological formation were joined by a new element—the mark of his daily relations with God, relations that were clearly not without vexation.

Critics have often contrasted the dark tone of these last sonnets with the buoyant "nature poems" that he wrote between "The Wreck of the Deutschland" and his move to Ireland in 1884. "Nothing is so beautiful as spring," Hopkins had exclaimed in 1877, and "Look at the stars! look, look up at the skies!" This is the sort of poetry that fits the Romantic ideology. But, as one Jesuit scholar points out, this "is not an indication that Hopkins is in any important sense a nature poet, a Catholic Descendent of William Wordsworth, so to speak; rather, the nature poems form a transition between the earlier ascetical spirituality . . . and the presence of Christ."[52] After 1884, the process by which Hopkins came to grasp the whole world—and himself in it—as sacramentally, inextricably infused by divine presence, forced nature into the background and his own humanity to the foreground.

About three months before he died in 1889, Hopkins composed Sonnet 74 (numbered thus in the fourth edition), "Thou art indeed just, Lord," which exemplifies more than any other single expression of his life his perception of the interdependence of his two vocations. The poem opens with a quotation from Jeremiah. In the Latin Vulgate Jeremias 12:1 reads, "*Justus quidem tu es, Domine, si disputem tecum: verumtamen justa loquar ad te*"; in the Douay-Rheims Catholic version, which Hopkins would have read, it is translated, "Thou, indeed, Lord, art just, if I plead with thee, but yet will I speak what is just to thee: Why doth the way of the wicked prosper? Why is it well with all them that transgress and do wickedly?" This is most similar to Hopkins' metrical translation of that verse in the first lines of Sonnet 74.

While on a retreat the year before he wrote this poem, Hopkins had noted:

> I was continuing this train of thought this evening when I began to enter on that course of loathing and hopelessness which I have so often felt before, which made me fear madness and led me to give up the practice of meditation except, as now, in retreat, and here it is again. I could therefore do no more than repeat "*Justus es, Do-*

mine, et rectum judicium tuum" and the like. . . . What is
my wretched life? Five wasted years almost have passed
in Ireland. I am ashamed of the little I have done, of my
waste of time, although my helplessness and weakness is
such that I could scarcely do otherwise. . . . All my un-
dertakings miscarry: I am like a straining eunuch. I wish
then for death; yet if I died now I should die imperfect,
no master of myself, and that is the worst failure of all.
O my God, look down on me.[53]

A few days later he wrote to Bridges, "all impulse fails me:
I can give myself no sufficient reason for going on. Nothing
comes: I am a eunuch—but it is for the kingdom of heaven's
sake."[54] He had given up the practice of meditation, out of
fear of madness, and now that he must meditate in retreat,
the result of his introspection is the question, "What is my
wretched life?" In the earlier Terrible Sonnets, Hopkins had
associated introspection with despair, darkness, wretched-
ness, gall, bitterness, sourness, thirst, eating carrion. The
progression of "I wretch lay wrestling with (my God!) my
God" to "God's most deep decree / Bitter would have me
taste" to "let joy size / At God knows when to God knows
what" (Sonnets 64, 67, 69) reveals the ongoing movement of
the consciousness of his own struggle with God's will, the
bitterness of self-determination, and the spiritual ideal of
detachment of will. By the time Hopkins writes Sonnet 74
he seems to have synthesized his relationship with God and
his own need to selve:

> *Justus quidem tu es, Domine, si disputem tecum;*
> *verumtamen justa loquar ad te: Quare via impiorum*
> *prosperatur?* &c.
>
> Thou art indeed just, Lord, if I contend
> With thee; but, sir, so what I plead is just.
> Why do sinners' ways prosper? and why must
> Disappointment all I endeavor end?

Wert Thou my enemy, O thou my friend,
how wouldst thou worse, I wonder, than thou dost
Defeat, thwart me? Oh, the sots and thralls of lust
Do in spare hours more thrive than I that spend,

Sir, life upon thy cause. See, banks and brakes
Now, leavèd how thick! lacèd they are again
With fretty chervil, look, and fresh wind shakes

Them; birds build—but not I build; no but strain,
Time's eunuch, and not breed one work that wakes.
Mine, O thou Lord of life, send my roots rain.

He sent this poem to Bridges in a letter dated March 20, 1889, about ten weeks before his sudden death.[55] One can imagine Bridges—established, wealthy, optimistic, leisured—attacking the sonnet for both its difficult style and distressing content, and one can imagine Hopkins being "rather bitter." Five weeks after this "dark sonnet," he sent "To R.B." a poem whose last lines are:

O then if in my lagging lines you miss

The roll, the rise, the carol, the creation,
My winter world, that scarcely breathes that bliss
Now, yields you, with some sighs, our explanation.

This turned out to be the last poem he wrote, and the last correspondence with Bridges: a touching, though unsuccessful, final attempt at explanation.

When Bridges wrote to Richard Watson Dixon on June 14, 1889, announcing Hopkins' death, he included a revealing postscript: "That dear Gerard was overworked, unhappy and would never have done anything great seems to give no solace. But how much worse it would have been had his promise or performance been more splendid. He seems to have been entirely lost and destroyed, by those Jesuits."[56]

How unjust that a life so rich and brilliant should seem "entirely lost and destroyed," not only to its bearer, but even to his best friend. This postscript of Bridges is a fitting gloss to his understanding of Hopkins' "terrible sonnets." In fact, though Hopkins suffered deeply from depression and poor health and frustration and exhaustion,[57] he insisted throughout that he felt himself to be in consonance with God's will, and that this feeling was to him better than "violets knee-deep." Not everyone personally experiences God's will, but Hopkins did, through discipline, intelligence, and no doubt grace. This plaintive sonnet is a monument to the personal integration of that experience with suffering.

God's justice often bewilders humans, for the rain falls on the just and the unjust alike. In *"Justus quidem"* Hopkins engages God in a colloquy, wondering why, if he as God's friend is defeated and thwarted, do sinners prosper? This is not the question of a jealous and self-righteous Pharisee, but rather of one who compares himself to the rest of nature and finds in himself stagnation and disappointment (in the spiritual life, this would be called dryness or aridity). Nature is productive: "banks and brakes" are "lacèd" with "fretty chervil" (cow parsley), "and fresh wind shakes them." No wind of inspiration helps speed the contending speaker, who spends life, strains, and does not breed. Birds build, but Hopkins has no nest. "Work that wakes," which he would like to breed, means not so much a work that will last, but one that arouses and will continue to have a life of its own separate from his weary self. Once again he refers to himself as a "eunuch." Still and dry, deprived of the fluency, lubrication, and flow of water, symbolic in nature (or in the Bible, where water is associated with God's blessing, cleansing, and baptism), he humbly, patiently, and plainly asks, "Mine, O thou Lord of life, send my roots rain."

The tone of this request and of this poem is not desperate, wretched, writhing, restless, or anxious, as was the tone of the previous dark sonnets. Emphasis falls on the word "Mine," implying Hopkins' possessive intimacy with the "Lord of life." And since *life*—vitality, growth, inspiration, and movement—is what he is requesting in "send my roots rain," and not the sleep of death of Sonnets 64, 65, and 67, this is surely a statement of hope. Previous intimations of hope and consolation invariably fluctuated and proved insufficient. But here, at last, at the very end of his career, his poetry becomes the mark of a great talent coming into alignment with a great will. Poetry is the sacrament of flesh, word, and spirit charged by their interpenetration with each other. When his resistance broke, Hopkins' highest gift was released.

CHAPTER TWO

"Charged with Grandeur": Hopkins' Use of Sacramental Language

During the late middle of the nineteenth century, when Hopkins was formulating his ideas, there were two philosophic traditions governing theories of language. The dominant one was based on rationalist epistemology, emphasizing that only clear, fixed, defined, and distinct perceptions could be true. Language must be precise in order to communicate those perceptions, and when language was used in religious or poetic ways, it tended to deceive. In fact, metaphor and symbol—as used in poetic and religious discourse—rendered language utterly meaningless. This "Cartesian" or "Benthamite"[1] or empirical idea of language gave rise to certain salutary notions and phenomena, including the English dictionary, which designates for words fixed and exact meanings. It also robbed words of what Malcolm MacKenzie Ross has called their "analogical reach."[2] Hopkins exercised rhetoric to the point where the flexibility of words, their stretch and "reach," could be restored. It was Hopkins' express intention that the reader be arrested by those qualities of words which were independent of their dictionary definitions. His use of language might be called "fiduciary,"[3] based on trust that his audience would respond to "excellences" that were higher than distinct definitions of words.

Sacramental language and poetic language share certain tasks. The divine manifests itself in concrete things through sacraments; poetry through such devices as symbolism and metaphor condenses an unseen reality into words. For Hopkins, who wished to use poetry to address, reveal, and praise God, poetic words shared the responsibility and power of sacramental words. For an orthodox Catholic, the words spoken over a sacramental action are not simply the conveniently chosen signs of a philosophy: they embody truths. For a poet who wishes to reconcile linguistic art with his convictions, poetic words must somehow embody what is true about the reality they describe.

In religion, the symbolic view of a sacrament—that it is merely a physical accident representing the substance of a divine truth—is naturally weaker than the view which presumes that the physical accident itself is the very truth, a view that would require a "fiduciary" response. Just as the fiduciary view of a sacrament requires that the believer consent to identify an element not only by its apparent *accidents* (bread, for example) but also by its unseen *substance* (body of Christ), likewise the fiduciary view of language requires a "complex act of inference and assent"[4] for words to bear meaning beyond their simplest referent. A sacramental response to language is not analytic, but relies on trust in analogical, symbolic, or metaphoric expressions. It entails a tacit agreement to find meaning in such turns of phrase as "Fair seedtime had my soul," "Poor soul, the center of my sinful earth," "I wake and feel the fell of dark," and "This is my body, broken for you."[5]

This "fiduciary" alternative to the "Cartesian" idea of language has been investigated by twentieth-century linguists, structuralists, and poetic theoreticians:

One of the most distinctive features of recent criticism has been its realization of the inherently ambiguous or polysemous nature of verbal discourse, and especially of poetic discourse. But this is something pre-Cartesian and pre-scientific in spirit, and if it does not immediately derive from, is at least compatible with, an approach to verbal exegesis which persisted from remote antiquity to the Renaissance and has played a not inconspicuous part in the reading of Christian revelation.[6]

The fiduciary alternative is embraced by all poets, and for the purposes of my argument, by Samuel Taylor Coleridge, and by the interacting literary and religious ideas of Hopkins. Coleridge and Hopkins, a Romantic and a Victorian, shared a profound devotion to the task of revealing in poetry the relation of the spiritual to the world of sense. The distinctions between them are more obvious than the similarities; simply, Coleridge was a Unitarian-tending Protestant and Hopkins a Roman Catholic. Subtler, and more appropriate to this discussion, is the way a common interest in relating the spiritual and the material required in Coleridge the use of symbolic language, and in Hopkins what I call sacramental language; and that this distinction proceeds ultimately from the conviction or opinion each held about the nature of religious sacrament.

Coleridge, who was interested in the coincidence of the poetic and the spiritual, was concerned with the poetic phenomenon wherein a higher reality is exposed to the human intellect through the poet's imaginative genius. Mr. Coulson points out:

Coleridge perpetuates the older, alternative tradition—that language is a living organism. . . . We begin by taking *on trust* expressions which are usually in analogical, metaphorical, or symbolic form, and by acting out the claims they make: understanding religious language is a function of understanding poetic language.[7]

In a predominantly empirical age, Coleridge insisted on the intimate relationship of language to human consciousness, and on the cooperation of thing and word. Language is "the medium of all thought to ourselves, of all Feeling to others, and partly to ourselves."[8]

"Coleridgean language," writes G. B. Tennyson, "is rather an attempt at synthesis whereby literary concepts are recognized to be aspects of a larger philosophic and theological unity."[9] For Coleridge as well as his companion Wordsworth, the natural points to the supernatural in an unbroken and continual relationship. "Nothing in Coleridge," says Tennyson, "has been so much quoted or so little pondered as the *religious dimension* of his definition of the imagination (italics mine). Most commentators seem to think that Coleridge *likened* the imagination to the infinite act of creation, whereas Coleridge said the Imagination was the *repetition* in the finite mind of the eternal act in the infinite mind."[10] In other words, Coleridge contributed to the revival of a pre-Benthamite tradition in which nature is infused with the supernatural, and artistic perception with religious significance.[11]

In his approach to the sacraments, Coleridge is said to have been "generally orthodox" and "faithful to the Thirty-Nine Articles."[12] The Thirty-Nine Articles are the code of the Church of England, composed in a time of reforming fervor and political stress, and in a spirit of compromise. They are not strict or precise doctrinal statements, and Article XXV, on the sacraments, reads:

> Sacraments ordained by Christ be not only badges or tokens of Christian men's profession, but rather they be certain sure witnesses, and effectual signs of grace and

God's goodwill towards us, by the which He doth work invisibly in us, and doth not only quicken, but also strengthen and confirm our faith in Him.[13]

In other words, the sacraments ordained by Christ (baptism and communion) are not mere "badges" as they were for the most radical reformers, but neither are they transubstantiated divinity. They are "signs of grace." Coleridge commented on the idea of the sacrament: "Here was the spiritual degraded into an image, and secondly, the image was unnaturally made to possess spiritual powers. . . . This is the character of superstition in all ages: it is the confounding of the spiritual with the bodily."[14] Here Coleridge revives the age-old anathema against "graven images" which the leaders of the final phase of the Reformation in England (under Cromwell) felt so keenly, and which anti-Roman opinion has always fastened on in its reference to "Popish foppery." The mixing of spiritual and bodily identities, which strikes Coleridge as an acceptable function for the imagination, qualifies as "superstition" when it includes the confounding of a religious image with spiritual power. John Henry Newman—who was to have a great influence on English Catholicism—suggested in his correspondence with James Stephen in 1836 that the whole Coleridgean position might be too ineffectual to counteract the danger that rationalism posed to religion. Coleridge, Newman pointed out, regarded "The Church, sacraments, doctrines, etc., rather as symbols of a philosophy than as *truths*—as the mere accidental types of principles."[15]

Catholic theology, from the time of the Church Fathers through the period of Scholasticism,[16] had repeatedly renewed the definition of the Sacrament of the Eucharist as the true body and blood of Christ. As God had entered the world as human flesh at the Incarnation, so he left himself to the world at the Last Supper. The Incarnation, death, and

Resurrection are commemorated at every mass, and the Incarnation is actually re-enacted as the bread and wine are transformed to flesh and blood. The effect of this sacramental pronouncement is objective, that is, valid *ex opere operato*—by means of the work itself, regardless of the dispositions of participating humans. The heretical position, dismissed throughout the Middle Ages, is *ex opere operantis:* that the sacrament is effective according to the disposition of the *worker.*

To generalize, Protestant reforms increased the emphasis on individual responsibility toward the sacrament, locating greater significance in the hearts and consciences of the recipients. The table in a Calvinist commemoration of the Last Supper was wooden and movable, and could be carried to the congregation of the faithful (the Catholic altar had always been of stone and unmovable, and the faithful came to *it*). It was a general ideal of eucharistic reforms to reduce those elements of magic or superstition associated with medieval sacramental beliefs.[17]

As a Roman Catholic, Hopkins endorsed transubstantiation of the Eucharist—while the material accidents of bread and wine maintained their original appearance, their substances became wholly the body and blood of Christ. In fact, it was this doctrine, he said, which most drew him to Catholicism: "The great aid to belief and object of belief is the doctrine of the Real Presence in the Blessed Sacrament of the Altar. Religion without that is somber, dangerous, illogical."[18] And later: "But I may for once speak . . . of the difference the apprehension of the Catholic truths one after another makes in one's views of everything, beyond all others those of course of the blessed sacrament of the altar."[19]

Hopkins accepted Catholic sacramental teaching and never used a poetic symbol. It would be too simple to say that Coleridge was a Protestant who rejected transubstantiation and therefore was a symbolist.[20] For one thing, Cole-

ridge's concept of a symbol had nothing in common with al-
legorical types. Natural symbols are *real* things, and their very
reality gives them sacramental meaning. And for Coleridge,
the human imagination had the power to create, perceive, or
mediate them: "By symbol, I mean, not a metaphor or alle-
gory or any other figure of speech or form of fancy, but an
actual and essential part of that, the whole of which it rep-
resents."[21] One could distinguish between simple or vertical
(iconic) symbolism, wherein one thing directly represents
another; and complex or simultaneous symbolism (mimetic),
wherein the symbol and thing symbolized participate in or
produce an imitation of a common reality. If Coleridge is in-
deed a symbolist, he is of the latter type, and for all his dis-
missal of the Catholic interpenetration of the sacrament, he
extols in literature *the capacity of genius* to unite two levels
of reality, the seen and the unseen.

The excellence of Shakespeare, argues Coleridge, con-
sists in a "union and interpenetration of the universal and
particular":

> In short, the material world has, in the human mind, a
> corresponding capacity in the senses and understanding.
> The universal has its counterpart in reason. And the crea-
> tive activity of nature, which unites universal and par-
> ticular, has *its* counterpart in the imagination, which
> "fuses" together the insights of reason with the impressions
> of the senses.[22]

For Coleridge, the *imagination* enjoys a quasi-sacramental
function, fusing the separate faculties of sense and reason
and finding words to embody that fusion. The human imagi-
nation becomes the source of a mysterious energy that can
fuse spontaneously form and matter, signifier and signified.
The Romantic symbol, forged by the imagination, has the
power to collapse distinctions between universal and partic-
ular, and to transcend the empirical view of the world as a

vast series of unconnected, helpless, inert parts. The Romantic imagination therefore enjoys the function of a mystical priesthood, binding a world of isolated subjects and objects into an experience of harmonious continuity.

Walter Pater, who was Hopkins' tutor at Oxford, said that the problem of post-Romantic—High Victorian and Pre-Raphaelite—poetry was that the structure of words had become extremely distant from the structure of the reality they tried to represent. He criticizes "aesthetic" poetry for being the opposite of "simple and spontaneous," for using "allegorical signs rather than participating symbols."[23] "Pater's symbols," observes J. Hillis Miller, "are a powerful vehicle of his description of the unnatural or even uncanny detachment from reality of aesthetic poetry."[24] "Aesthetic poetry satisfies a desire for escape from any actual form of life into some artificial realm or 'earthly paradise.' "[25] Pater, who presumably exerted tutorial influence on Hopkins, saw the artistic problem as one of harmonizing the dissonance of reality and art, matter and form: "All art constantly aspires toward the condition of music. For while in all other kinds of art it is possible to distinguish the matter from the form, and the understanding can always make this distinction, yet it is the constant effort of art to obliterate it."[26]

The matter or subject of a poem by Hopkins seemed to determine the rhetorical form it would take, according to the "inscape"—the deep unity—of what he perceived. This has left him open to a range of criticism. Some critics have accused him of "mannerism," though ironically, his poetic practice was nothing if not an effort *against* mannerism, preciousness, and escapism. J. Hillis Miller notes that Hopkins attempted "to reintegrate the disintegrated through linguistic inscapes"; he attempted to "repair the disaster of Babel. . . . Hopkins' poetic problem was to communicate the incommunicable. It was an attempted rescue of the self and language through language."[27] Critics unprepared for the full force of Hopkins' effort could be upset, aesthetically, by the poetry that resulted:

> The fatal sophistication in Hopkins, the touch of just-too-muchness in his words, rob one of the sense of fulfillment and make one wonder what he is really trying to say. . . . His words go out in pursuit of reality like falcons stooping to the kill; and there is a destructive effect in the contact, a bruising on impact that leaves the object stunned with the force of the word.[28]

Given his acceptance of the doctrine of the Real Presence, Hopkins could never employ words—especially words with religious or eucharistic overtones—to make a simply decorative or pantheistic figure. In Hopkins, the literalness of Catholic sacramental doctrine met a literal epistemology and an often "unaesthetic" choice of poetic language. In a letter to Bridges he explained his use of "shook foil" in his sonnet "God's Grandeur," which begins, "The world is charged with the grandeur of God. / It will flame out, like shining from shook foil":

> I mean foil in its sense of leaf or tinsel, and no other word whatever will give the effect I want. Shaken goldfoil gives off broad glares like sheet lightning and also, and this is true of nothing else, owing to its zigzag dints and creasings and network of small many cornered facets, a sort of fork lightning too. Moreover as it is the first rhyme, presumably it engendered the others and not they it. This reminds me that I hold you to be wrong about "vulgar," that is obvious or necessary, rhymes. It follows from your principle that if a word has only one rhyme in the language it cannot be used in selfrespecting poetry at all. The truth seems to me that a problem is set to all, how to use that same pair (or triplet or any set) of rhymes which are invariable, to the finest and most natural effect. It is nothing that the reader can say/He had to say it, there *was* no

other rhyme: you answer/shew me what better I could
have said if there had been a million. Hereby, I may tell
you, hangs a very profound question treated by Duns Sco-
tus, who shews that freedom is compatible with necessity.[29]

The question of how belief in Catholic sacramentalism
informs an *ars poetica* enjoys some precedent in literary crit-
icism. In his discussion of seventeenth-century English po-
etry, M. M. Ross has emphasized the relationship between
literary language and the dogmatic changes brought about
by the Protestant Reformation.[30] The Protestant interpreta-
tion of the sacraments, which divested the Eucharist of its
transubstantial nature, and the continuing growth of skepti-
cism about the reality and knowability of universals, are
both seen to have important consequences for poetry. Chau-
cer and Dante, according to Ross's argument, had in com-
mon a set of beliefs that made their poetry necessarily more
"sacramental"—their art more closely related to their beliefs,
and their allegories and analogies more successful because
more simultaneous and organic—than the work of Spenser
and Bunyan.

The physical accidents of a sacrament are visible, but its
character is invisible. We cannot see the body of Christ sac-
rificed on the altar; therefore, it is understood analogically.
Radical Protestantism tried to reduce this kind of analogy to
an immediately accessible symbol, according to Mr. Ross.
The intuitive relationship between the two parts of this anal-
ogy, he argues, was weakened, and thus the reach of symbol
in poetry also became abbreviated.

The Incarnation is *the* type of a sacrament, for in it God
entered created reality by means of a sign. Through the In-
carnation, the world is redeemed and restored to dignity,
and thus dignified, a thing may take on spiritual meaning
without losing its specific, concrete meaning. The complex
identity of a sacramentalized "thing" stands in contrast to

the simplified, reduced "symbols" of a purely rational order. A poetic allegory in which an emblematic, flat character exists solely to bring to mind some higher virtue or event necessarily represents a reduction of the power of Chaucer's or Dante's full, complex characters, who bear spiritual meaning without losing their earthly meaning. By extension, the sacrament must be real not only in heaven, but on the altar of the parish church. "A denial of the Real Presence and real sacrifice," says Ross, "is inevitably a denial of . . . the sanctification of natural things . . . and an assault on the analogical validity of poetic symbol."[31]

In his study of the nineteenth-century expressions of this "de-sacramentalized" universe, J. Hillis Miller says:

> The Eucharist is the archetype of the divine analogy whereby created things participated in the supernatural reality they signified. Poetry in turn was, in one way or another, modeled on sacramental or scriptural language. The words of the poem incarnated the things they named, just as the words of the Mass shared in the transformation they evoked. . . . The history of modern literature is in part the history of the splitting apart of this communion.[32]

Against this de-sacramentalization and dissociation in theological and artistic expressions, the nineteenth century produced various reactions, including the Oxford Movement and the Pre-Raphaelite movement. For Hopkins, use of language as functioning boldly, directly, even as part of the subject of a poem, was parallel to the Pre-Raphaelite use of color in painting as radically functional in itself, and not merely a medium.

The revival of the power and significance of emblems, allegories, and symbols can be related to the revival of sacramental doctrine associated with the Oxford Movement. To state the terms of this revival briefly, before the Reformation

religious language itself—for example, the words of the con-
secration at mass, "This is my body"—had power to trans-
form what it referred to. The growth of science in the seven-
teenth and eighteenth centuries, an increasingly empirical
approach to language, and the Protestant concept of the
sacraments gradually sapped this power. Just as the Oxford
Movement represented, in part, an effort to restore super-
natural interpretation to the sacraments, the Pre-Raphaelite
poets entertained the conscious goal of restoring "sacramen-
tal" content to the language of poetry. But, as Humphry
House points out, it was arguably Hopkins and not the
so-called aesthetes who developed the aims of the Pre-
Raphaelites.[33]

As a Victorian, Hopkins inherited not only the Protestant
definition of a sacrament, but also the new—and for many,
the vexatious—theories of evolution and of entropy. The the-
ory of evolution and how Hopkins absorbed it shall be dis-
cussed briefly in the next chapter. Entropy (molecular dis-
order, but also thermal energy that is being lost and not
replaced), and for that matter energy in general, Hopkins
himself commented on in his philological and metaphysical
inventiveness. At the same time, Hopkins inherited a set of
mid-nineteenth-century assumptions about meter and poetic
structure—Wordsworth and Tennyson were the poets laureate
during his youth—that his particular theological formulations
helped him to challenge.

The concept of entropy, that energy was running out of
the universe, was troubling to Victorians who had counted
on the beneficent and constant presence of a divine Creator.
Furthermore, entropy contradicted the idea of a divine or-
der. Belief in the sacrament of transubstantiated bread and
wine provided Hopkins with a reversal of this: the localiza-
tion of divine energy into these two physical elements estab-
lished order of a special sort, and added to, did not subtract
from, the amount of energy in a given system:

> The transformation of bread and wine into body and blood provided a model for change that served as an alternative to the physicist's model of thermodynamic decline. In the transubstantiation there is a change from a lower to a higher state of charge instead of the reverse; therein lay the action of grace.[34]

The Incarnation, which is re-enacted every time bread and wine are consecrated and transubstantiated, carries energy *into* the physical world from outside. A closed system becomes charged *upward*. Hopkins uses the language of physics: "charge" and "discharge" as in "The world is charged with the grandeur of God" ("God's Grandeur") and "Thence the discharge of it" ("Wreck"). His prose is filled with the imagery of heat, stress, and pitch. At the end of his career he recognized in poetic form that, although "nature's bonfire burns on" and "world's wildfire, leave but ash," the Resurrection is a clarion to the heart. These lines, from "That Nature is a Heraclitean Fire and of the comfort of the Resurrection," take up the notion of the pre-Socratic philosopher, Heraclitus, that fire is the basic physical element. The Heraclitean fire consumes everything, but somehow recycles and restores what is consumed. In Hopkins' poem, clouds, wind, pool, ooze, dust, crust, all are fuel for "nature's bonfire." Even nature's "bonniest, dearest . . . clearest-selvèd spark / Man" is quickly gone and forgotten, and "all is in an enormous dark / Drowned." It is a terrible pity, "But vastness blurs and time ǀ beats level." All of the physical elements of earth are consumed and forgotten, but the Resurrection, "heart's-clarion," joyful news to the heart, restores everything "in a flash, at a trumpet crash." Because of the Incarnation, in which God became poor flesh, the destructive oxidation of time's passing and eroding is reversed: "time ǀ beats level." Then, far better than being an earthly element, "I am all at once what Christ is, ǀ since he was what I am," and resurrected, both are "immortal diamond."

"For Hopkins, 'stress' means the supporting pressure of divine animation as well as metrical emphasis."[35] He connected the instress of the natural world with the order of poetic expression. Highly charged language was a corollary of his highly charged beliefs, and of his way of considering created nature:

> By contemplation of simple objects—flowers, trees, streams and landscapes—Hopkins was at times raised to ecstasy, because he realised that the hidden energy (instress) moulding things into shapes, patterns and colours (inscapes) was the very energy of God himself. This outward and visible beauty was to him the reflection of the energy and invisible beauty of God. So in this sense all nature was sacramental to him—the visible sign of an invisible, intelligent and creative energy.[36]

Sprung, hard-stressed rhythm was his way of charging each poetic line with the maximum of energy, in imitation and praise of what he perceived in nature—nature, that is, supported by the Incarnation and promise of Resurrection. Sprung rhythm was the opposite and antidote to the enervated, predictable, one might almost say, entropic meters of "Parnassian" verse.[37]

Hopkins declared that the poetic language of an age should be "the current language heightened,"[38] and he usually chose idiosyncratic methods to heighten current language. The basic materials of his methods were short, non-Latinate words, arranged in "sprung rhythms." Hopkins did not invent sprung rhythm, as W. J. Ong has pointed out; neither did he derive it from a tradition. He *found* it in human speech.[39] Hopkins never chose a cliché or a ready expression. To generalize experience would be to falsify it. He wrote to his friend:

> I cut myself off from the use of *ere, o'er, well-nigh, what time, say not* (for *do not say*), because, though dignified,

they neither belong to nor ever cd arise from, or be the elevation of, ordinary modern speech. For it seems to me that the poetical language of an age should be the current language heightened and unlike itself, but not (I mean normally: passing freaks and graces are another thing) an obsolete one. This is Shakespeare's and Milton's practice and the want of it will be fatal to Tennyson's Idylls and plays.[40]

Many critics have shown Hopkins' meter to have ample precedent in English poetry, comparing it especially with Milton's:

Hopkins:

The World is charged with the grandeur of God

Milton:

By the waters of life, where'er they sat

Hopkins:

Look at the stars! look, look up at the skies!

Milton:

Light from above, from the fountain of light.[41]

Hopkins himself defended his sprung rhythm as rigidly restricted, and his zeal in proving this is impressive:

And my quantity is not like "Fiftytwo Bedford Square," where *fifty* might pass but Bedford I should never admit. . . . I never allow e.g. *I* or *my* (that is diphthongs, for $I = a + i$ and $my = ma + i$) in the short or weak syllables of those feet, excepting before vowels, semi-vowels, or *r*, and rarely then, or when the measure becomes (what

is the word?) molossic. . . . If you look again you will see. So that I may say my apparent licenses are counterbalanced, and more, by my strictness. In fact all English verse, except Milton's, almost offends me as "licentious." Remember this.[42]

He proves not only that his choices of poetic diction are thoroughly considered, but that they are part of a program that is greater than the concerns of pure rhetoric. The compression, piling on, listing, alliteration, consonant-chiming (called in Welsh, from which Hopkins learned the technique, "cynghanedd") were not only sound patterns, but amazingly often, patterns of logical meaning. He discovered patterns of fascinating linguistic harmonies ("shadow, shade, shed, shelter, shield"; "skim, scum, squama, scale, keep"; "shear, shred, potsherd, shard"),[43] but these were lists of potential materials, and no more. When these materials became poetry, they appeared in an exact context and order that evoked and even reproduced the reality they described.

Some words express relationship to experience by onomatopeia (cluck, whirr), or by a more complex imitation of an action or quality (peal, brittle, rustle, whistle, creep, shiver). Still subtler, however, are words that are not imitative but are in some way psychologically or musically suggestive, such as glitter, swoon, mood, horror, jelly.[44] From this last category Hopkins, like most poets, chose much of his poetic vocabulary, and then organized words in a way which, as Herbert Read asserts, required "Nice discernment." Consider the synonyms *flood* and *deluge:*

"The horror of an universal *deluge*" is right; and "being like the poor sinners at Noah's *flood*" is right—the one, I think, because the epithet "universal" requires a bed of soft sound on which to fall, and the other because the open sound of "Noah's" requires a bank of firmness to contain them.[45]

Hopkins carried this intuitive sense of quasi-musical composition to an extreme, wrestling with words to inscape an idea or justify a particular word to a particular image right before the reader's eye. For example, the first lines of "To What Serves Mortal Beauty?":

> To what serves mortal beauty ╎ —dangerous; does set
>   dancing blood—the O-seal-that-so ╎ feature, flung
>   prouder form
> Than Purcell tune lets tread to? ╎ See: it does this:
>   keeps warm
> Men's wits to the things that are; ╎ what good means—
>   where a glance
> Master more may than gaze, ╎ gaze out of countenance.

This energetic search for the strong, no-nonsense stress imitates the particular energy of the Incarnation discharged into nature, when the divine entered a particular, localized human. At the Incarnation the body and blood of the human child of Mary was the body and blood of the Son of God; at the consecration the sacramental elements are stressed in the same way; Hopkins' poetic language imitates this charge of divine energy when that language is most exacting, vital, and particularized.

For most Victorian poets, as for the Romantics,[46] nature is the setting for the discovery of truth. To the "beauteous forms" of nature, Wordsworth owed, as he wrote in "Tintern Abbey," such gifts as "that serene and blessed mood," in which

> we are laid asleep
> In Body, and become a living soul;
> While with an eye made quiet by the power
> Of harmony, and the deep power of joy,
> We see into the life of things.

The typical pattern of a Victorian or Romantic poem about nature and what it awakens in the human mind includes a descriptive beginning followed by an interpretation. In a sonnet the octet describes some natural phenomenon, the sestet its higher meaning. Hopkins' sonnets follow this Romantic pattern, but the higher meaning is always the supernatural God. The perception of the "freshness deep down things," however, is immediate, active, never elegiac. It epitomizes the Jesuit ideal of contemplation in action and demonstrates the sacramental beliefs of the poet in the apparent interpenetration of energy, or spirit, and matter. In this Hopkins diverges from the Romantic poets: "What to Wordsworth or Turner or Thomas Hardy might seem natural accident within an indifferent universe, the priest must proclaim as the act of God: he understands that the God who is, is terrible: 'And here the faithful waver, the faithless fable and miss.'"[47] If one compares Hopkins' sonnet "The Starlight Night," with "Frost at Midnight" by Coleridge (whose program for reviving a pre-Cartesian or fiduciary use of language found an intuitive follower in Hopkins), one can see the effect of Hopkins' particular grasp of the interpenetration of nature and supernature.

> Look at the stars! look, look up at the skies!
>   O look at all the fire-folk sitting in the air!
>   The bright boroughs, the circle-citadels there!
> Down in dim woods the diamond delves! the elves'-eyes!
> The grey lawns cold where gold, where quickgold lies!
>   Wind-beat whitebeam! airy abeles set on a flare!
>   Flake-doves sent floating forth at a farmyard scare!
> Ah well! it is all a purchase, all is a prize.
> Buy then! bid then!—What!—Prayer, patience, alms, vows.
> Look, look: a May-mess, like on orchard boughs!
>   Look! March-bloom, like on mealed-with-yellow sallows!
> These are indeed the barn; withindoors house

The shocks. This piece-bright paling shuts the spouse
Christ home, Christ and his mother and all his hallows.

This sonnet, written in what Hopkins called "my Welsh days, in my salad days," exemplifies not only his fascination with peculiar metrical forms[48] or even his happy enthusiasm for the natural beauty of Wales, but his perception of the charge of energy in natural things. The earliest draft of his sonnet, "God's Grandeur," which begins, "The world is charged with the grandeur of God," was dated February 23, 1877, and "The Starlight Night" is dated one day later, February 24. Both poems carry the theme of natural beauty, charged with divine meaning, revealing *and* hiding the face of God.

The octet of the sonnet commands the attention of the listener, who is ordered, "Look . . . ! look, look . . . ! / O look . . . !"; and in a series of exclamations of excitement, a stage of stars is compared to gatherings of mythical folk, towns, castles, wood-sprights, branches of trees aflame, and barnyard fowl scurrying. None of these metaphors or personifications predicts a pious conclusion. Besides, stars are visible only at night, and only on some nights, and even then they move around and flicker. Like the material world of towns, citadels, and farms to which he compares these arrangements of stars, their very motion which makes them exciting also makes them unstable and given to chance: "Ah well! it is all a purchase, all is a prize."

The sestet takes up the language of purchasing and reward, imitating an auctioneer: "Buy then! bid then!" The cost of the purchase that one would want so much is "Prayer, patience, alms, vows." The currency of spiritual virtues would buy one not only flickering physical beauty, however, but eternal beauty. After setting the price in the first line of the sestet, Hopkins invites us once more to *look* at the stars. These are seasonal references—to spring and bloom but also

to harvest and feasting. This time the metaphors do have re-
ligious overtones—orchard boughs like a May-mess (Mary-
mass), yellow-dusted sallows (perhaps pussy willows) like
March-bloom (the flowers of Lent). "These are indeed the
barn," whether these be stars or the flowers, the "bright bor-
oughs," "circle-citadels," "diamond delves," "elves'-eyes"[49] to
which he compares them. Nature thus is a barn—a rustic
shelter, a place of storage. This barn, this empty tabernacle,
this rude temple, houses "the shocks," which like most of
Hopkins' poetic images can mean various things: shocks or
loose bunches of grain, sudden impacts, or even electric
charges. The bright "paling" (fencing) of this particular
barn shuts home "the spouse/Christ," and the Blessed Vir-
gin, and the saints. By shutting them home, it *contains* them,
gives them a location. This sonnet begins with a rhetorically
intense linking of images and personifications; it ends by see-
ing not only a starry sky but all of nature, which becomes a
bright enclosure for Christ, Mary, and the saints.

Coleridge's long, mature, meditative poem, "Frost at Mid-
night," makes much different use of the material offered by
a winter night. Where Hopkins' descriptions are breathless,
compressed, at times even incoherent, Coleridge's are dis-
cursive, meditative, and tranquil. Hopkins' sonnet is not a
discourse, but a cry, or at its calmest, a liturgical incanta-
tion. Coleridge concludes that the shapes and sounds of
nature are the language of God, "who from eternity doth
teach / Himself in all, and all things in himself. / Great uni-
versal teacher! he shall mould / Thy spirit, and by giving
make it ask" (ll. 61–64). The means, however, by which this
language reaches human understanding differs for both Cole-
ridge and Hopkins. For Hopkins, that language is charged
into nature by the divine, and is understood by the human
perception of inscape. For Coleridge, only the genius of po-
etic imagination can read this language.

"Frost at Midnight," like many of Coleridge's poems,

bears the tone of something recollected in tranquillity. To aid the powers of recollection, Coleridge kept meticulous, unsentimental notebooks of his observations of nature, which remind one of the notebooks of Hopkins. Compare Coleridge on a stone-crop flower:

> exactly a star . . . 6 petals equi-distant, most tender & delicate purpose, with a white ground as it were, attempting to gleam thro it / and the little round of the o in the centre of the flower are of the darkest crimson, very far darker than the barbery shaped leaves. (2.2564.)[50]

And Hopkins:

> Honeysuckle at the hedge on the big bank in bloom, the crests coiled back into a crown, the tongues or spurs curled at heel, the lashes (anthers) giving off all round: this is their time of greatest beauty.[51]

Or again, Coleridge:

> What a beautiful Thing Urine is, in a Pot, brown yellow, transpicuous, the Image, diamond shaped of the Candle in it. . . . (1.1766.)[52]

And Hopkins:

> The slate slabs of the urinals even are frosted in graceful sprays.[53]

For Coleridge, a description carefully noted is a prelude to the intense perception that will lead to poetry. We must look at a natural phenomenon accurately, and see it as itself in all its exactitude. Poetic genius enjoys an imagination developed to perceive, and then to enter with even greater penetration into the heart of a thing. This second and deeper level of seeing will yield an intense emotion which—when recollected in tranquillity—can be expressed to others using metaphor, simile, personification, and heightened diction. The language of common speech can still be cast into beautiful poetry.

Hopkins' letters and journals contain some of the same jagged, stark turns of style which, in poetry, might become sprung rhythm. Yet, one almost never finds an entry in the journals which, later recollected, appears in a poem. The observations in Hopkins' journals seem rather to be for their own sake, as though his interest in them *must* find some expression. Furthermore, his interest is often quite scientific. For pages Hopkins reports nothing in his journal but weather:

> AUG. 5.   Sunlight dim; radiations in the sky at night.
> AUG. 6.   Rain at last.
> AUG. 7.   Dull morning; threatening afternoon, with some rain.[54]

There are some eccentric, by no means uncharacteristic, notes:

> APRIL 27—Went to see Saulty Abbey (Cistercian): there is little to see
> Mesmerised a duck with chalk lines drawn from her beak sometimes level and sometimes forewards on a black table. They explain that the bird keeping the abiding offscape of the hand grasping her neck fancies she is still held down and cannot lift her head as long as she looks at the chalk lines which she associates with the power that holds her. This duck lifted her head at once when I put it down on the table without chalk. But this seems inadequate. It is most likely the fascinating instress of the straight white stroke.[55]

At one point Hopkins sent a very long letter to the British journal, *Nature*, concerning "The Red Light round the Sun— The Sun Blue or Green at Setting," in which he provided a most careful report of his sightings of colors in the sky around the sun, with nothing that could be called poetic elaboration.[56] Then in 1875, the year that he was to resume writing poetry, his journal abruptly ended.

"The frost performs its secret ministry," Coleridge's poem begins, "Unhelped by any wind." This personification of frost, and of wind as its potential helper, is set in a quiet meter that Hopkins might have struck only in his latest and most subdued poems, and never in a poem that was primarily about the effects of nature on the soul. The next few lines of "Frost at Midnight" point out the major difference between the tranquil meditation of Coleridge and the sharp immediacy of Hopkins' reports:

> The inmates of my cottage, all at rest,
> Have left me to that solitude, which suits
> Abstruser musings: save that at my side
> My cradled infant slumbers peacefully.
> 'Tis calm indeed! so calm, that it disturbs
> And vexes meditation with its strange
> And extreme silentness. (ll. 4–10)

The prose-like sequence with its dependent clauses, the repetition of synonyms ("disturbs / And vexes," "strange / And extreme") while like the lulling sequence of Wordsworth's lines, would never have found space in a poem by Hopkins. Coleridge concentrates more on the philosophy of the poem than on the senses and what they can perceive. The action of this poem takes place entirely within the poet's mind and soul and in their combined faculty, the imagination; a film fluttering on his fire-grate is "the sole unquiet thing" in his cottage, and in the setting of the poem. It seems to be, above all, a poem about the relationship between the outer world and the inner, mediated by the poet's quiet voice. Addressed to *"thou*, my babe!" the poem promises the "cradled infant" that when he is growing up, he will "wander like a breeze / By lakes and sandy shores, beneath the crags / Of ancient mountains," and by constant conferences with nature and its "lovely shapes and sounds," the infant will learn "that eternal language, which thy God / Utters." The word "quiet" appears twice in the last line.

Philosophy and the senses conspire in Coleridge to unlock a higher level of experience, which has to do with "Feeling" and at its best is expressed in poetry.

> Coleridge, then, though not devaluing the world of sense phenomena, is consigning it to a subsidiary role in the all-important quest for the expansion of human self-consciousness and the divination of an inner moral cohesion in the universe. Until a thing is a symbol, it is to Coleridge less than itself; until it takes its place for him as a word in God's "language of nature," it is deficient.[57]

The quest for "the expansion of human self-consciousness and the divination of an inner moral cohesion" was satisfied for Hopkins by instress, inscape, and the necessary harmony of a universe where divine energy *itself* was localized every single day, in every single celebration of the mass, in the transubstantiation of bread and wine. Moral cohesion was not "inner" for Hopkins, but was a function of the Incarnation, which charged divine significance into the world of sense.

Hopkins' grasp of harmony or cohesion is not simply a hope for the reconciliation of some thread of opposites, or for some thread of meaning running through all things. The *locus* of meaning in this case would be the human mind that had been gifted enough or fortunate enough to make the connections, whether through genius or effort. Hopkins' harmony, his inscape, is not an accident of human intelligence—it is *there,* it has been charged by God. The evidence of divine presence in nature is the Catholic interpretation of the sacrament. Hopkins' poetic language, while making no direct reference to the theological truths of sacramental teaching, nevertheless repeats the immediacy, the energy, and the localization of meaning *outside* of and *away* from the poet's own imagination. "Look at the stars! look, look up at the skies!" he commands. The sacramental focus is always in an element outside of the individual soul.

Just as Hopkins wrote "The Starlight Night" in his "salad days," Coleridge wrote "Frost at Midnight" in his heyday. Later, Coleridge suffers from "dissociation of sensibilities"; in "Dejection: An Ode," he writes, "I see, not feel, how beautiful they are." This is the polar opposite of the feeling of instress, where the nature and order of a thing are impressed totally on all of the human faculties. In the same poem Coleridge writes, "I may not hope from outward forms to win / The passion and the life, whose fountains are within" (ll. 45–46). And Hopkins had his own period of dejection. Whereas Coleridge suffers dejection from the blurring, opacity, and density of physical being, Hopkins continues to recognize and envy the vitality of the physical world outside of his suffering self: "See, banks and brakes / Now, leavèd how thick! lacèd they are again / With fretty chervil, look, and fresh wind shakes / Them; birds build—but not I build." Coleridge seems always to want to charge upward, to transform the material to the spiritual, using his own poetic imagination as the source of energy. His grasp of the material world and its meaning is subjective. For Hopkins it is objective; the world is already charged.

While for Coleridge imagination enjoys the sacramental function of fusing sense and reason, for Hopkins sacramental action is something that can occur only outside of his own imagination. And although both poets use language in a "fiduciary" way, in faith that their audience will agree to find meaning in non-rational formulations, Hopkins' reasons for this are explicitly Catholic. Regardless of the individual's capacities and perceptions, the power of the sacrament is *ex opere operato*, residing within the work itself:

Hopkins delights in the revelation of the distinctive self, he cherishes the sensation of it, but he combines this Romanticism with a preference for the unselfconscious spontaneity of being, in which the joy of recognising the statement of personality belongs to the spectator not the exponent. There is an objectivity at the heart of his approach to self which distinguishes him from his predecessors.[58]

Hopkins was allowed this objectivity by the presence of sacramental energy to such a degree that "nature is never spent; / There lives the dearest freshness deep down things." The soul may be spent by dejection and fatigue, but the eternal offer promised at the Incarnation, the "vein / Of the gospel proffer, a pressure, a principle, Christ's gift," is constantly repeated and renewed.

CHAPTER THREE

Unravelling Reality: Hopkins' Theology of the Particular

A description of transubstantiation as a repetition of the Incarnation, not symbolically but really, opens the old question of the status of particulars and their relationship to the universal. The problem of universals had consumed the attention and energy of many Scholastic thinkers who pondered whether universals actually existed or were simply terms composed of nothing but the sound of the voice uttering them, and if they existed, what relation they bore to the particulars in nature which exemplified them. The doctrine of transubstantiation implied that a natural particular could contain the obvious material accidents of one thing (bread, for example) and the formal substance of another (Christ). In the nineteenth century, after centuries of philosophic and philologic progress, the question of the relation of particulars to universals was more or less dismissed by the assumptions of empirical positivism—that *only* concrete particulars, perceived by the senses and registered by reason, existed, and that universals were *terms*, mere words, invented for the convenience of categorization. How did Hopkins, an alert Victorian, adjust this view of a world of apparently unrelated particulars to a sacramental concept?

Hopkins never was a poet of vague uncertainties, projecting his emotions on the objects of his eye or of his mind's eye. With astonishing accuracy, his language corresponded to each object's sum of qualities. Sometimes the reader is expected to suspend disbelief in Hopkins' descriptions, such as "worlds of wanwood leafmeal lie," and to assent to his intuitive empathies with nature and the proper way to write about it. His instincts were almost always those of an exacting naturalist, thriving in a Victorian golden age of naturalists. But Hopkins was undeniably different from other Romantic, Victorian, and especially Pre-Raphaelite poets whose empathies and instincts might *appear* to be similar to his. Each thing in nature was marked by what Scotus called "thisness" (*haecceitas*), which connected it—if we could intuit the exact sense of "thisness"—to the universal, to God. All words and the objects that words exist to tell of, rhyme, chime, and share something because all derive from the same universal original Logos. Thus Hopkins sensed that intense visual attention and sensory passion could be connected to faith. If he looked very hard not at himself but at *things,* they would reveal to him something about their source and creator and would become in fact a means of prayer and praise:

> Whatever is fickle, freckled (who knows how?)
>   With swift, slow; sweet, sour; adazzle, dim;
> He fathers-forth whose beauty is past change:
>
> > Praise him.

What was absolutely novel in Hopkins' writing was this startling, sustained double vision: he saw God in particulars, particulars in God.

Hopkins' view of nature absorbed not only that of the Romantic poets, but that of Darwin. Duns Scotus' concept of *species specialissima* offered some theological implications for Darwin's idea of the origins of species. Nineteenth-century naturalists who either predated or rejected Darwin's ideas[1] could interpret natural elements as allegories, or symbols, or utilities to remind the soul of God. But for Hopkins, they were

> divine concrete realities; and to middle-protestant moral-ity Hopkins the Catholic would much have much pre-ferred Philip Gosse the Plymouth Brother and fundamen-talist, lamely and sincerely ejaculating over his marine animals: "Yes, O Lord! the lovely tribes that tenant these dark pools are, like the heavens themselves, 'the work of thy fingers,' and do as truly as those glowing orbs above us 'declare thy glory.' "[2]

The existence of individual species perfectly suited the strict, piercing habit of religious discernment Hopkins adopted. Natural objects did not *remind* him of God, as they might have reminded the Neoclassic or Romantic poets, they *were*, in a sense, God.

The medieval epistemological question regarding the ex-istence of universals had been given a positivist answer by the mid-nineteenth century. At the time of the twelfth-century revival of dialectic, the Realist or Platonic position on the question was that universal concepts did exist, *before* the particular things which might embody them (*ante rem*); the moderate position held that universals existed only *within* individuals, that form and matter, accidents and substance, were coincidental and inseparable (*in re*); and the nominal-ist position was that universals did not exist except as con-structions of the imagination, which invented categories for individual objects of perception that shared common traits (*post rem*). Nominal universality (positivism) characterized late Victorian epistemology; only what could be known by the senses could be true; the essence of each thing could be found only in its individuality; accidents *were* essence.

Hopkins might have appeared to treat accidents as essential:

> Perhaps his insistence on physical fact, his bringing of all existence to the test of the incarnational here and now of this world made Hopkins seem so much one of themselves to the positivists of Cambridge in the 1920s. Yet in nothing is he more Catholic than in the sacramentalism of his physicality.[3]

Hopkins' sacramental "physicality" proceeded mostly from his understanding of the status of sacrament as distinct from symbol and revealed his effort to harmonize the details of the physical world with God. On a literary level, he did this through his concepts of rhyme, inscape, stress, and selving. And he chose a kind of poetry that was served by sinewy, thumping, visceral rhythms and by a vocabulary of compounded, invented, and recovered English words. He needed an alternative, even a contrary language, to express the pointedness and particularity of his perceptions.

The medieval problem of universals became a nineteenth-century problem partly by way of the philosophy of empiricism and partly by way of the implications of Darwin's findings.[4] For Hopkins, the relationship of the particular to the universal was direct because of the Eucharist, in which both inhered at once, and because of the Incarnation, to which the Eucharist referred as its original type. Usually, in the history of philosophy, the perception of particulars has forced the concept of a universal God to recede. Hopkins drew God back into natural objects by his sacramental spirituality and by the significance that a sacramental identity gave to particulars.

"The change from verbal to visual genius," wrote one scholar, "is one of moment for the nineteenth-century mind. It symbolizes the growing prestige of objects and the growing obligation of the beholder to behold."[5] Consider Words-worth's "Tintern Abbey": in his youth, "colors and forms" were "all in all" to him, and there was "no delight unborrowed from the eye." Later, recollecting these colors and delights, the poet's imagination transformed them and released their "higher" meaning. "O Christ, it maddens me," wrote Coleridge in his notebook, "that I am not a painter or that Painters are not I!"[6]

> Thus Coleridge expresses his frustration at being unable to convey in words what he sees on the Scottish tour with the Wordsworths in September 1803. The exclamation is revealing in various ways: it suggests the intensity of his study of landscape and its features, his desire to preserve and communicate what he looks at.[7]

It seems that with the development of science there was an extroversion of the observer's mind onto nature. Sentimentality about nature was gradually being replaced by acute, empirical observations such as we see in Hopkins' notebooks, which are a continual log of particulars. So too are Coleridge's. Still, for Coleridge all nature was a series of symbols pointing to God, while for Hopkins nature was a series of discrete particulars, isolated by their ontological status as separate entities. And both their uses of language diverged accordingly.

The Catholic concept of sacrament never lost its localization in particular elements the way the Protestant concept of sacrament did after the Reformation. In the Tridentine Mass, the words "this is my body" referred not only to a particular body, but to its localization in a particular element at a particular moment. In the Calvinist communion, the sacramental action took place in the hearts of those faithful who were present. This diffusion, according to the Catholic apologist Johann A. Möhler (*Symbolik*, 1832), was responsible for the weakening of the Protestant concept of sacrament into a quasi-pantheist sign. Partly through his Catholicism and partly through his understanding of particulars, Hopkins departed from the tradition of Wordsworth and Coleridge, and from the generation of Newman and Kingsley who could see no meeting place for science and poetry. In Hopkins we see reality grasped with a mind and an eye at once medieval and modern.

For Hopkins the particular identity of individual creatures and the particularity of the presence of Christ in the Eucharist were inseparable. Christ entered the world as God entering a natural particular, as *word* in which all things were created or incarnated. The Incarnation was the central Catholic principle necessary to the doctrine of the Real Presence. Hopkins wrote to his father when he was twenty-two, "This belief once got is the life of the soul and when I doubted it I should become an atheist the next day."[8] To a college friend he had written in the same year, "I think that the trivialness of life is, and personally to each one, ought to be seen to be, done away with by the Incarnation."[9] Coleridge had claimed that the imagination had the power to transform particulars; for Hopkins it was the understanding of the Incarnation that could, in an intuitive flash, inform a particular object with transcendent significance. Any particular that served as a poetic image for Hopkins revealed through its nature the reality of Christ. *Haecceitas,* the epistemological term he borrowed from Scotus, might also be called infinite particularity, that is, "thisness" which connects essentially to God.

Hopkins was not effusive in his praise and appreciation of his great predecessors, with the exception of the thirteenth-century Franciscan, the "Doctor Subtilis," Duns Scotus (1265–1308). In 1872 Hopkins wrote in his journal,

> At this time I had first begun to get hold of the copy of Scotus on the Sentences in the Baddely library and was

flush with a new stroke of enthusiasm. It may come to
nothing or it may be a mercy from God. But just then
when I took in any inscape of the sky or sea I thought of
Scotus.[10]

In defending his choices of poetic diction, he wrote to Brid-
ges, "Hereby, I may tell you, hangs a very profound question
treated by Duns Scotus, who shews that freedom is com-
patible with necessity."[11] In contradistinction to Aquinas,
Scotus had indeed emphasized the primacy of free will over
knowledge and reason. "I care for him more than Aristotle,"
Hopkins said, "and more *pace tua* than a dozen Hegels."[12]

Unlike his Franciscan predecessor Bonaventure, Scotus
held that one could move inductively from particulars to
generals, that the mind—without noting the transitions into
the associations and acquired mental mechanisms that occur
between the perception of a particular ash tree and the in-
tuition of "treeness"—could discern "an exact and progressive
conformity between the nature of an individual object and
the nature of the universe."[13] All beings, spiritual and corpo-
real, shared "prime matter" (*prima materia*) and thus, de-
spite the multiplicity of *forms* that occurred in nature, *mat-
ter* was held in common. In addition to form and matter,
creatures enjoyed a "principle of individuation" (*haecceitas*).
Humans could intuit "an exact and progressive conformity"
between individuals and the universal because of common
prime matter; all being was in a sense univocal. The stamp
of individuation or particularity was impressed on creatures
by God, and the unaided human reason could perceive this.

Aquinas claimed that we could know reality only reflex-
ively and/or indirectly; Scotus, that we could know it di-
rectly. For Scotus, each being is not a mere reflection of a
greater Being—although each thing is one of and within the
One, each thing nevertheless has a *self*. Spiritual reality can
be absorbed directly through the senses because we have an

innate memory whereby we intuit the original or common nature of things before they were individualized. That is, we may perceive the unique nature of a particular thing (ash tree) behind which is a common nature (treeness), behind which is God, who created it all ("past all / Grasp God"). God has ideas of all created things, but nature became real only in individuated things. Hopkins would say that when the human can perceive God's intention behind each thing, this is the perception of inscape, and that all things, containing God's energy, express themselves and make themselves known to us:

> All things therefore are charged with love, arc charged with God and if we know how to touch them give off sparks and take fire, yield drops and flow, ring, and tell of him.[14]

Hopkins did not have to choose whether to endow things with significance or to leave them unendowed; in a sacramental universe all nature was a web of significance. Present in Hopkins was the tension between the Victorian linguist, who would consider the word as a name for an object, and the Christian Realist, who would consider the word itself an object, since from Creation and Incarnation to the minutest thing that could be named, all derived from the Divine Word:

> To every word meaning a thing and not a relation belongs a passion or prepossession or enthusiasm which it has the power of suggesting or producing but not always or in every one. This *not always* refers to its evolution in the man and secondly in man historically.[15]

The sacramental view of nature and its absorption into poetic language made the most of this tension: for Hopkins, things did not act as symbols, and words were not merely symbols, except in the most unavoidable sense. Words were treated as particulars, as rooted in nature, as visceral, organic, direct. "The strength of a symbol is its truth on all levels, including the physical."[16] But just as the Church localized the sacrament in a particular element, for Hopkins each poetic image was precisely located: "There would no doubt be something revolting in seeing the heart alone, all naked and bleeding, torn from the breast, but Christ's heart is lodged within his sacred frame and there alone is worshipped."[17]

"Man's spirit will be flesh-bound when found at best" ("The Caged Skylark"). Earth, matter, flesh give things being by making them particular. Hopkins compares the Blessed Virgin to the very air that surrounds and supports us:

> Wild air, world-mothering air,
> Nestling me everywhere,
> That each eyelash or hair
> Girdles; goes home betwixt
> The fleeciest, frailest-flixed
> Snowflake; that's fairly mixed
> With, riddles, and is rife
> In every least thing's life.

As air is "mixed / With" life, human flesh becomes mixed with God, riddled and rife with divinity, when Mary makes God particular at the Incarnation in "The Blessed Virgin Compared to the Air We Breathe":

> Through her we may see him
> Made sweeter, not made dim,
> And her hand leaves his light
> Sifted to suit our sight.

Hopkins expended less energy on the semantic power of words (to refer, to name) than on the syntactic, that is, on the power of words to function within the environment of other words, using rhyme and rhythm to force words away from their purely referential roles and to draw attention to their "wordhood," their substantial quality. By endowing words with substance and energy, Hopkins gave them "passion or prepossession or enthusiasm,"[18] and the enriched nature of a sacramental element. Words have this potential and power "but not always or in every one";[19] rather, only where they have been handled so as to fulfill their potential, that is, in certain poetry. This poetry must be inventive and inspired, presenting a pure and rare impression of what it means. "Every true poet," Hopkins wrote, "must be original and originality a condition of poetic genius; so that each poet is like a species in nature . . . and can never recur."[20]

Hopkins' use and understanding of language was in a constantly creative state. Words did not abide by the prescription of rigid rules; they were not fixed concepts whose identities could be impaired by the breaking of a particular syntactic habit.[21] Yet, although Hopkins was willing to use words ambiguously, to stretch them to the limits of their phonetic, grammatical, and semantic capacities, he did perceive in language the same order and regularity that he saw in nature. To Hopkins, "words are like other creatures: they have inscapes beautiful in themselves"[22]

In his early notebooks (1865) Hopkins composed a "Platonic dialogue" called "On the Origin of Beauty" in which he first presented his notion of rhyme:

> which is a short and valuable instance of my principle. Rhyme is useful not only as shewing the proportion of disagreement joined with agreement which the ear finds most pleasurable, but also as marking the points in a work of art (each stanza being considered as a work of art) where the principle of beauty is to be strongly marked, the intervals at which a combination of regularity with disagreement so very pronounced as rhyme may be well asserted. . . .

> . . . rhyme is the epitome of your principle. All beauty
> may by a metaphor be called rhyme. . . .[23]

The "principle" of this rather brilliant undergraduate essay
is that all beauty depends on a recognition of the likeness
between things which are not similar, on a perception of pat-
tern or design no matter how recondite. A world of unre-
lated and isolated particulars is given sense by this principle,
which recurs in Hopkins' retreat notes fifteen years later:
"Any two things no matter how unlike are in some things
like."[24]

In that early essay which claimed that "all beauty may
by a metaphor be called rhyme," Hopkins distinguished be-
tween chromatic beauty (where the pattern or rhyme is
marked by gradual, sliding change) and diatonic beauty
(marked by sudden change). He showed a preference for
diatonic beauty even at that point, and did not waver
throughout his life in his taste for the distinct, the irregular,
the sudden, and the stressful: "All things counter, original,
spare, strange; / Whatever is fickle, freckled." However, what
he defended in his essay "The Probable Future of Meta-
physics" (1867) as "fixed" or "Platonic" species, he later
came to defend, in terms of the Incarnation, as having or-
ganized particulars within divine creation. First, in the early
essay he says: "To the prevalent philosophy and science
(evolutionism) nature is a string all the differences in which
are really chromatic but certain places in it have become
accidentally fixed and the series of fixed points becomes an
arbitrary scale."[25] Hopkins came to object explicitly to the
sense of chance and arbitrariness in "the prevalent philoso-
phy and science"; years later he wrote in his retreat notes:
"Nothing finite can determine what itself shall, in a world
of being, be. . . . It always in nature's order is after the
nature it is of."[26]

The first step in Hopkins' lifelong effort to make aesthetic and theological sense of a world of unrelated particulars was his conversion to Roman Catholicism. There followed many years of poetic silence during which he carefully ordered, collected, and recorded details. One scholar, reviewing the art of Ruskin and the Pre-Raphaelites, considered the metaphysical implications of a taste for exact detail:

The detailed representation of even the smallest objects in each painting makes each one a possible focus of contemplation. The paintings thus imply a symbolic view of the world, in which each object can become instinct with meaning. By thus singling out each object, the Pre-Raphaelites build into their painting stylistically the impetus to a sacramental view of reality. At the same time the naturalism of the portrayal pushes what had been a symbol toward status as a natural object, the sheer quantity of detail pulls it back toward status as a symbol. . . . Faced with a world of natural objects instinct with symbolic meaning, man can understand that meaning by intensity of contemplation. The conscious elaboration of detail in Pre-Raphaelite art reveals just such a consciously symbol-making effort. Far from producing a fatal lack of integrity of focus, the combination of allegorical and highly realistic details suggests the process of symbolic perception.[27]

The defense of "fixed species" and of the Platonic or Realist position by Hopkins probably draws intuitively on Ruskin's theories, which he knew, and certainly offers an interesting balance to his apparent treatment of accidents as essence. Species *must* be real or fixed, for God *must* be the patterning and organizing force. For Hopkins, the sense of the absolute precision not only of details but of the pattern between them, of the unity of an individual object determined by God and perceived by humans, of the convergence of parts in several objects no matter how apparently diverse or opposite, of repetition, of rhyme—all of these were *inscape*. Hopkins' responsibility as a highly "pitched," individuated creature was to *instress* this accurately.

The first appearance of the words "inscape" and "instress" was unaccompanied by definition; Hopkins makes this statement instead: "nothing is so pregnant and straightforward to the truth as simple *yes* and *is*." Yet the impulse that invented terms like "inscape" and "instress" contained the inclination to embellish the simple words yes and is. At this time in his life (1868), when Hopkins was formulating the philosophic background to what would become an interlocking system of theology and poetics, he was writing of Parmenides:

> His feeling for instress, for the flush and foredrawn, and for inscape / is most striking and from this one can understand Plato's reverence for him as the greatest father of Realism. . . . But indeed I have often felt when I have been in this mood and felt the depth of an instress or how fast the inscape holds a thing that nothing is so pregnant and straightforward to the truth as simple *yes* and *is*.[28]

Being in the Parmenidean system is univocal, that is, it has the same quality for creator and creature, for each of the sides of any equation. Hopkins continued in his notes on Parmenides:

> Without stress we might not and could not say/Blood is red/but only/This blood is red/or/The last blood I saw was red/nor even that, for in later language not only universals would not be true but the copula would break down in particular judgments.[29]

The *copula*—what in English would be "is"—bears the burden of stressing the univocity of blood being blood, and its being red. Here Hopkins addressed anew the problem of universals and of how language refers to them. The copula connects two particular things or qualities. When Jesus held up the bread at the Last Supper and said, "This is my body," could the copula (or the Aramaic equivalent) hold up under the stress of bread *being* body? In subsequent celebrations of the Roman Catholic Mass, did the phrase "*hoc est corpus meum*" empower "*hoc*" and "*corpus*" to *be* univocally? Language in the Realist (or Parmenidean) system had to express universals; for Hopkins it had to express *inscape,* that is, universality and particularity *unified* in a precise identity. Language had to bear sacramental power. In other words, "transubstantiation, the central mystery of the Catholic faith, must in its nature transform the whole world . . . the Parmenidean 'it is' becomes, in the vision of the cosmic Christ, the Biblical 'I am.' "[30]

Rhyme and inscape established relationships between words, between words and the things they stood for, and between particular things and the universal, or God. Rhyme and inscape took on sacramental functions the way symbolism did for other poets. I cannot think of any poem in which Hopkins used a direct symbol, and this was because the particularity of an object, its selfhood, must be significant as it stood. A falcon, for example, was *not* something other than itself. It was being and acting as itself in "The Windhover" and in the imagination of the poet that perceived the rhyme, or relationship, between it and the sublime. The intuitive empathies of the poet released distinct, specific words to communicate, inimitably, something about that relationship. The poem was dedicated "to Christ our Lord," but there is no reason to conclude that the bird was a symbol, direct or indirect, of the crucified or risen Christ. Nature was for Hopkins, as Plotinus put it, "the poetry of God." Down to the least separable part, the individuality of phenomena must inhere in poetry, as in nature. This creative energy directed at *minutiae* as well as at grand patterns was the very opposite of the flabbiness, the mechanistic "Parnassian" poeticism, the sentimentality, subjectivity, and false facility that Hopkins chose constantly to avoid.

For Hopkins, only in concreteness could an object reveal anything about being—and being had the same quality for a particular as for a universal. Simultaneously to be, and to be individual, Hopkins called "selving." Only God could bestow on and sustain the action of selving in a finite thing. The predetermined individual nature of a thing was sustained by divine grace:

> Now to be determined and distinctive is a perfection, either self-bestowed or bestowed from without. In anything finite it cannot be self-bestowed: nothing finite can determine its own being, I mean its being as a whole; nothing finite can determine what itself shall, in a world of being, be. . . . It always in nature's order is after the nature it is of.[31]

Humans are the most distinctive, most highly "selved" of creatures. Hopkins used the term "pitch," as both a noun and a verb, to discuss highly selved and inscaped things. A human is "pitched" or intentionally thrown at a certain "pitch" or level of determination. Humans, however, have personality, which is distinct from human nature (which exists prior to the individual human's existence). For Hopkins, personality is moral freedom to decide one's destiny. Personality requires a human nature in order to display itself—just as accidents require substance to become incarnate, or the heart needs a body to enclose it. And although one's personality is predetermined by one's creator, one has free will:

> This intrinsic freedom may be called "freedom of pitch"; but it needs "freedom of play" in the natural faculties in order to display itself. . . . Pitch is a pre-existing deter-

mination of man towards his eternal destiny by his creator, but in such a sort that the man is left free to determine himself. . . . This is where the priority of pitch to existence is all-important. There is a world of *possible* being prior to existence, in which God sees and loves a man fulfilling God's will and achieving his own destiny. God is able to illumine a man's mind and affect his will with the sense that he *already* is this nobler, consenting self. . . . But . . . man is free to make a leisurely avowal or disavowal.[32]

Using the word "pitch" where Scotus would have used "haecceitas" ("Is not this pitch then or whatever we call it the same as Scotus' *ecceitas?*"[33]) or individuality, Hopkins must concede to the Scotist position that pitch can exist only in an existing substance. The more distinct and determined that pitch is, however, as it must be with humans, the more reality it has apart from the nature in which it dwells. A highly pitched human—one for whom God has prevenient intentions—has a distinctiveness that separates him or her from human nature. He or she becomes more idiosyncratic, unusual, particularized. Hopkins here reflects, perhaps unconsciously, not only on his sense of God's high expectations for him, but also on his sense of lonely and separate eccentricity: "When I compare myself, my being-myself, with anything else whatever, all things alike, all in the same degree, rebuff me with blank unlikeness; so that my knowledge of it, which is so intense is from itself alone, they in no way help me to understand it."[34] The particular pitch of a highly selved creature is exhilarating to observe and consider, and lonely to experience.

Scotus makes a formal distinction between a thing's nature and its individuality. What separates things is the *especial* degree to which they possess their common nature. In a human, greater individuality means a greater distance from the infinite. This distance is felt and perceived as *stress*.

Humans are the most stressed creatures in nature. Stress pushes and pitches them toward the infinite. It keeps individuality *in being*.

Stress has been defined as "the ictus of being flowing from the world of objects, their knowability as projectiles of thought; it is the bridge of juice through the stem of things, which impels us to acknowledge Being."[35] Stress is the presence of divine power pent up in all creation; Christ is the most stressed, has the most *being* of any creature. The more distinctive a thing is, the more it is stressed; the more it is stressed, the more it presses toward the Infinite and has Being. "The sense of pressure or stress is the sixth and radical sense in Hopkins."[36] In his lecture notes on rhetoric, he defined stress as being "like weight":

> Now every visible, palpable body has a centre of gravity round which is its balance and a centre of illumination or *highspot* or *quickspot* up to which it is lighted and down from which it is shaded. The centre of gravity is like the accent of stress, the highspot like the accent of pitch, for pitch is like light and colour, stress like weight.[37]

Christopher Devlin points out how unlikely an intellectual guide Duns Scotus must have been:

> Gerard Hopkins at one period of his life, 1875–79, drew his poetry almost entirely from Nature. In this he appears to have been aided by Scotus, for in 1875 he wrote "I was flush with a new enthusiasm. Whenever I took in an inscape of the sea or sky, I thought of Scotus." To anyone who has taken in an inscape and then opened a page of Scotus this remark should come as a shock. For Scotus presents at first nothing but a mass of bristling syllogisms. Nevertheless behind this barrier savagely guarded is the sleeping beauty. That is why Scotus is not served in the ordinary course of scholastic philosophy. Scholastic philosophy must not go beyond what the average man with

the unaided use of reason can attain; for a scholastic to appeal to private inspiration would be ludicrous. Actually Scotus knew this and never does appeal beyond reason. But he achieves his effect by hiatuses—. . . . Knowledge ceases on the threshold that Desire may enter in: he warns you about that at the beginning of his book.[38]

"Hiatuses"—the breaks, caesurae, and sprung pauses between stressed moments—were exciting to Hopkins. He found in Scotus a companionable spirit, though Scotus required that Hopkins himself become "the rarest-veinèd unraveller" of reality.

From his youth Hopkins seemed inclined to this philosophy. His diaries and letters reveal a steadfastly sincere, pure, and honorable young man with charming eccentricities. He was an amateur linguist and nature enthusiast:

Wade, waddle, vadere, vadum.
wade : waddle = stride : straddle = swathe : swaddle . . . etc.[39]

Snakes'-heads.
Like drops of blood. Buds points and like
snakes' heads, but the reason of name from
mottling and scaly look.[40]

His microscopic powers of observation were obvious in the landscape sketches published with the journals. His early notebooks addressed the question: What is the nature of visible things? He rejected the creative experience of seeing. Already far from the Romantic notion that the poet's eye gives nature a special character, Hopkins' eye *realized* reality. At twenty-one he had recorded:

Sunset here also. Over the nearest ridge of Dartmoor. Sky orange, trail of Bronze-lit clouds, stars and streak of brilliant electrum underneath, but not for this, but effect of dark intensified foreground. Long rounded ridge of Dartmoor deep purple, then trees on the descending hill, and a field with an angle so that the upper level was lighter green the lower darker, then a purplish great brown field, then the manufactory with grey-white timbers (it is built of wood) and grey shingle (?) roofs.[41]

At thirty his interest had not flagged, though Hopkins claimed that the "zest in the mind" did:

Blue shadows fell all up the meadow at sunset and then standing at the far Park corner my eye was struck by such a sense of green in the tufts and pashes of grass, with purple shadow thrown back on the dry black mould behind them, as I do not remember ever to have been exceeded in looking at green grass. I marked this down on a slip of paper at the time, because the eye for colour, rather the zest in the mind, seems to weaken with years, but now the paper is mislaid.[42]

His desire to grasp, in his life and his poetry, reality in its every detail without recourse to fantasy, allusion, or abstraction, his obsession with "stress," as well as the special perceptions he sought, all caused him frustration and nervous upset. He wrote in his journal,

One day in the Long Retreat (which ended on Christmas Day) they were reading in the refectory Sister Emmerich's account of the agony in the garden and suddenly I began to cry and sob and could not stop . . . if I had been asked a minute beforehand I should have said that nothing of the sort was going to happen.[43]

Later, on seeing some ash trees cut down, Hopkins wrote that he felt a terrible pang "and I wished to die." He claimed to regret his eccentricity: "It is the virtue of design, pattern or inscape to be distinctive and it is the vice of distinctiveness to become queer. This vice I cannot have escaped."[44]

Yet, however he felt about his own distinctiveness, he actually defended and abided by the solitude of his particular artistic gift. This produced a conflict, explicit in the poems and in the devotional writings, since the isolation of self-centeredness and willfulness is an offense against the Ignatian rule. He admired the "lovely ease of change of place" of birds and clouds, and prayed, "let me be to thee as a circling bird." But he always sensed the urgency, the insistence of human selfhood and its resistance to surrender, and its disharmony with other creatures and with God. It became *necessary* for Hopkins to resolve the conflict between his taste for the distinctive and his will to discern, obey, and fit in with God's will. To some critical eyes, his appreciation of the particular came across as exactly what he wished to avoid, egoism:

> Hopkins' theory and practice point in one direction. Put together such recurrent terms as "inscape," "sublime," "distinctiveness," "masculinity," "character," and one is forced to the conclusion that it was just this, Milton's egotism, individualism and arrogance, which made him for Hopkins, the model poet. His own poetry and his own criticism proceed from the single assumption that the function of poetry is to express a human individuality in its most wilfully uncompromising and provocative form. His is the poetry and the criticism of the egotistical sublime.[45]

Hopkins interpreted his own distinctiveness, and his taste for it in other things, as a mark of being "highly pitched." The stress of a high pitch was toward God: the more a thing was isolated by its particularity, the more it would strive to share in the infinite.

In "Ribblesdale" Hopkins contrasted the nonhuman, "Earth, sweet earth, sweet landscape . . . / . . . heaven that does appeal/To, with no tongue to plead, no heart to feel" with the human, "To his own self-bent so bound, so tied to his turn." Since nonhuman nature lacked soul and intellect or what might be called "heart," it could strike between its parts an easy harmony unavailable to humans, those more highly pitched creatures. The "heart" was the essential quality of being human—capable of suffering, but more distinctive and more alive because of it; as Hopkins expressed in "The Wreck":

> Ah, touched in your bower of bone
> Are you! turned for an exquisite smart,
> Have you! make words break from me here all alone,
> Do you! —mother of being in me, heart.

In a sermon, Hopkins again contrasted the human capacities with those of the rest of nature:

> The sun and the stars shining glorify God. They stand where he places them, they move where he bid them. "The heavens declare the glory of God." They glorify God, *but they do not know it.* The birds sing to him, the thunder speaks of his terror, the lion is like his strength, the sea is like his greatness, the honey like his sweetness, they are something like him, they make him known, they tell of him, they give him glory, but they do not know they do, they do not know him, they never can, they are brute things that only think of food or think of nothing. This then is poor praise, faint reverence, slight service, dull glory. Nevertheless what they can, they *always* do. . . . *But man can know God, can mean to give him glory.* This then is why he was made, to give God glory and to mean to give it.[46]

And in his retreat notes he again associated stress with pitch, with both leading to "selving"; "pitch is the distinctive and distinguishing feature of self: 'Nothing else in nature comes near this unspeakable stress of pitch, distinctiveness, and selving, this self-being of my own.' "[47]

The balance or relationship between individuality and unity in the process of perception is a constant tension for Hopkins. He had a strong sense of personality and seemed disinclined to imitate other figures. He wrote to Bridges, "The effect of studying masterpieces is to make me admire and do otherwise."[48] Often scrupulous in his observance of the Ignatian ideal of *quasi-cadaver* (to be as a body without will, or in the classic image of the Christian tradition, to be used "as an old man's staff" in the hands of God or God's viceroy), yet participating in what may be called an ideal of perfectionism, especially regarding the perfectibility of the self, it often seemed clear that humility was something he sought rather than naturally or easily possessed. Hopkins reflected on the human, the most selved being:

> When I consider my selfbeing, my consciousness and feeling of myself, that taste of myself, of *I* and *me* above and in all things, which is more distinctive than the smell of walnutleaf or camphor, and is incommunicable by any means to another man (as when I was a child I used to ask myself: what must it be to be someone else?). Nothing else in nature comes near this unspeakable stress of pitch, distinctiveness, and selving, this selfbeing of my own.[49]

In his poetry the experience of selfhood is in fact often "unspeakable" and agonizing: "Untwist the strings, the last strands of man in me, most weary cry, I can no more"; "My own heart let me more have pity on"; and "God's most deep decree / Bitter would have me taste: my taste was me": all of these lines express the poet's efforts to discover an easier disposition for his own personality in relation to God and to detect the inscape of himself as a creature.

In the spring of 1879 Hopkins wrote a sonnet about his favorite distinctive personality, Duns Scotus. Yet, in the poem, one is struck by how little is said about the personality of Scotus himself.

Duns Scotus's Oxford

Towery city and branchy between towers;
Cuckoo-echoing, bell-swarmèd, lark-charmèd, rook-racked,
    river-rounded;
The dapple-eared lily below thee; that country and town
    did
Once encounter in, here coped and poisèd powers;

Thou hast a base and brickish skirt there, sours
That neighbour-nature thy grey beauty is grounded
Best in; graceless growth, thou hast confounded
Rural rural keeping—folks, flocks, and flowers.

Yet ah! this air I gather and I release
He lived on; these weeds and waters, these walls are what
He haunted who of all men most sways my spirits to peace;

Of realty the rarest-veinèd unraveller; a not
Rivalled insight, be rival Italy or Greece;
Who fired France for Mary without spot.

What Hopkins admires in Scotus is not *his* originality or distinctiveness, but rather that his is "a not / Rivalled insight," and that he is "of realty the rarest-veinèd unraveller." Scotus perceives and unravels the distinctive details of things; reality to him is *haecceitas* or individuality, intuited through the senses. But not even this fact is made clear in the poem.

As with nearly all of Hopkins' sonnets, the octet delivers a series of descriptive particulars and the sestet, the universals induced from them. The octet in this sonnet describes Oxford, first with the Miltonic adjectives "towery" and "branchy," then with a line of jangling, sprung, Hopkinsian compounds that inscape the physical presence of Oxford. "That country and town did / Once encounter in" describes an older, more balanced, Catholic Oxford. Now, the "graceless growth" of industrialism and brick suburbs sours and confounds what used to be "Rural rural keeping"—"keeping" meaning the distinct, maintained atmosphere. Philip Endean suggests that this Romantic prejudice against the "base and brickish" industrial settlement which surrounds or skirts and therefore "sours" Oxford's grounds, and the Wordsworthian preference for nature untouched by any modern human ingenuity (medieval ruins are fine), is a sign of the incompleteness of Hopkins' sacramentality. Ironically, it was probably his encounters with Duns Scotus that enlarged his sense of the divine presence in creation to the degree that, after 1874, he ceased to use the term "inscape" in favor of a tacit assumption of total sacramentality.

In the sestet Hopkins begins "Yet ah!" for to his surprise and relief, he is reminded that the same air, weeds, waters, and walls were in Oxford when Duns Scotus lived there. In this revelatory part of the poem, Hopkins turns his attention from Oxford to himself and to Duns Scotus, "who of all men most sways my spirits to peace," because Scotus vindicated the certainty of knowledge through the senses. Hopkins calls him "rarest-veinèd unraveller," and the Church labelled him "Subtle Doctor." Hopkins implies that not even Thomas Aquinas ("Italy") or Plato or Aristotle ("Greece") can rival his insights. Furthermore, Scotus had "fired France for Mary without spot"—an apparently peculiar conclusion, except that in 1879, when Hopkins was writing this poem, the Church was celebrating the twenty-fifth anniversary of the Immaculate Conception proclaimed as dogma by Pius IX. Scotus, against the arguments of several generations of Dominicans, had gone to Paris in 1301 to argue in favor of the doctrine that Mary was conceived without original sin, and that it was necessary for her to have been free of sin to receive the Incarnate God. In a sermon on the Immaculate Conception, Hopkins, with his own dogged patriotism, refers to Scotus:

It is a comfort to think that the greatest of the divines and
doctors of the Church who have spoken and written in fa-
vour of this truth came from England: between 500 and
600 years ago he was sent for to go to Paris to dispute in
its favour. . . . (This) wise and happy man by his an-
swers broke the objections brought against him as Samson
broke the thongs and withies with which his enemies tried
to bind him.[50]

The current running through this sonnet is a recognition of
Oxford's natural beauty, which today has soured. The subtle
distinctions that Scotus made there, when its "grey beauty"
was grounded entirely in "neighbor-nature," might well be
confounded by the "base and brickish skirt" that surrounds
the town now. A good place to discern the distinctive in-
scapes of the divine is in nature, which is pure and stainless.

The particularity of what Hopkins said in his poems re-
vealed more about his theology than most of his carefully
groomed arguments: the poems stressed out his faith. Each
poem became a *credo,* with words as sacramental elements,
his experience as the transcendent force, and Hopkins him-
self as the celebrant.

CHAPTER FOUR

"So Arch-especial a Spirit":
Hopkins as a Baroque Poet

Hopkins' attention to the particular and to the separateness, oppositeness, and distinctiveness of things, his preference for what he called the "fickle, freckled," his position as a Catholic in a largely anti-Catholic society, the exuberance, vigor, explosiveness, sensuousness, spectacle, and multiple tones of his rhetoric, place him in a tradition that I should like to call baroque. The term baroque usually designates a European style in the arts of the late sixteenth and seventeenth centuries, between Renaissance and Neoclassic. Heinrich Wölfflin considered it a "degenerate" style. He also suggested some links between the visual arts and poetry. Wölfflin compared the light, cheerful language of Ariosto's *Orlando Furioso* (1516) with the baroque style of Tasso's *Gerusalemme Liberata* (1584).[1] The baroque poetry he noted was heavily rhymed, repetitious, ponderously constructed, and grand—images of laurel wreaths were replaced with "a golden crown of everlasting stars." Like many writers on the baroque, Wölfflin saw it as the decay of the Renaissance, as degeneration and dissolution parallel to that which characterized the period of the Fall of Rome.[2]

97

Even the etymology of the term bears tones of reprobation. *Baroco*, claimed Benedetto Croce, is the source for the word meaning the fourth mode of the second figure in the nomenclature of syllogisms in Scholastic proofs,[3] implying that the artifice and strain of late Scholasticism has something in common with the extremity of baroque ingenuity and ornateness. Another theory holds that the word comes from *barroca*, a Portuguese jewelers' term for an imperfect and irregular pearl. René Wellek points out that "in the eighteenth century the term emerges with the meaning of extravagant, 'bizarre.' "[4] Associated with the Counter-Reformation and the Jesuits, baroque art and literature carry the taint of casuistry, political intrigue, and the unsavory public image of the Catholic Church during what it perceived to be a time of siege. In fact, its early critics called it the art of the Counter-Reformation[5] and associated it usually with Jesuits and entirely with anti-Protestantism. Its voluptuous embodiment of the religious imagery loathed by the Calvinists and Zwinglians was seen as an expression of rebellion against reform.

It is true that the period of history designated as baroque was marked by an intensification of Protestant-Catholic conflict. During this time the Jesuits enjoyed their period of greatest growth, influence, and geographic spread; the Council of Trent and its aftermath reasserted the central authority of a universal Church in the face of Protestant efforts to undermine those qualities; Trent further emphasized the importance of strict form and visible ritual. Even in architecture, Wölfflin saw a reflection of these facts in "a quickened pulse" between the decorative units of a church, with "interiors and exteriors shouting loudly at one another." Wölfflin dictated the four essential marks of baroque style in the visual arts: (1) painterliness, which replaced a linear style and produced the illusion of movement; (2) monumentality, love of the grand, the massive, and the awesome; (3) multiplication of members or units making up a whole; (4) movement, lack of repose.[6]

In his exacting and scholarly essay on baroque as a literary designation, René Wellek first claims that "it is probably necessary to abandon attempts to define baroque in purely stylistic terms" and that one should then try to see it as "a term for a definite period."[7] He does admit, however, that there may be baroque "stylistic devices" which might be "considered symptomatic of a specific state of mind, if it expresses a 'baroque soul.' "[8] Wellek concludes that it is possible to define baroque using "analyses which would correlate stylistic and ideological criteria."[9]

Vitality, mobility, multiplication or repetition of parts within the whole—these are qualities of Hopkins' work as well. He is baroque in an extrahistorical sense, in his sensibility and in his relationship to Jesuit ideals. As a Jesuit in a Protestant country at the time of the First Vatican Council (which had certain goals in common with the Council of Trent over 300 years before), Hopkins shared some circumstances with the Jesuits of the Counter-Reformation. "The Wreck of the Deutschland" ends with a prayer to the drowned nun for a "Reward: / Our King back, Oh, upon English souls!" Many an Elizabethan Jesuit was executed for devoting himself to the reconversion of England. In "To What Serves Mortal Beauty?" he refers wistfully to Pope Gregory the Great's decision to send a mission to Anglia: "But God to a nation I dealt that day's dear chance."

Considering the atmosphere of anti-Catholicism that dominated England after the Reformation period and extended into much of the Victorian age, Hopkins had more in common with a Jesuit of the baroque age than might seem initially obvious. "British anti-Catholicism," wrote one scholar,

> though it had obvious points of similarity with European expressions of ideological objection to Catholic beliefs and

practices, was quite unique. It was peculiarly related to popularly subscribed precepts about the ends and nature of the British state; it was chauvinistic and almost general.[10]

With the passing of Catholic Emancipation in 1829 (which allowed English Catholics to vote), a consistent tradition of anti-Catholicism reaching back hundreds of years once more became a matter for public debate. In the 1840s English public attention was occupied by the question of support for Maynooth, the Catholic Seminary in Ireland. In 1850 Cardinal Wiseman was established at Westminster—the first Roman Catholic cardinal to preside in England since the Elizabethan Reform—and a cry went up against "papal aggression." The events of Vatican I, especially the dogmatic declaration of papal infallibility, excited great hostility. And as the Anglo-Catholic movement within the state church gathered force, British fear, suspicion, and loathing of converts, effeminacy, superstition, crucifixes, genuflections, vesting of clergy, and so on, brought Catholicism under renewed attack. In 1875 Foxe's *Book of Martyrs,* complete with an illustration of the Massacre of St. Bartholomew in which sixteenth-century Huguenots were dispatched, was reissued to a Victorian audience with whom it was nearly as popular as the Bible: "The Massacre of St. Bartholomew, together with numerous other tableaux on similar themes, belonged to a tradition of anti-Catholicism whose wide acceptance and long endurance, among all classes in society, secured it an important place in Victorian circles."[11]

In addition to this accident of sociology, Hopkins' rhetoric and poetic theory are defensibly baroque. His preference for the "fickle," the irregular, not only in nature but in his poetic techniques, represents a baroque tendency. "Poetry is speech," he wrote in his journal, "which alters and oftens its inscape, speech couched in a repeating figure."[12] To borrow an architectural term, Hopkins used the pointed rather than the plain style. Musically, sprung rhythm is analogous to counterpoint or the contrapuntal of baroque composition. Hopkins always insisted that his poetry was above all musical: "Read it with the ears."

> And since the new or mounted rhythm is actually *heard* and the mind at the same time supplies the natural or standard foregoing rhythm, . . . two rhythms are in some manner running at once and we have something answerable to *counterpoint in music*, which is two or more strains of tune going on together.[13] (Italics added.)

Others recognized this in Hopkins, calling him "an accomplished composer of fugues, who aimed to utilize in his language the most telling correspondence between sound and sense, and to give his compositions in verse an ordering comparable to the intricacies of counterpoint."[14] Hopkins may have loved the irregular "pied" things for the way they necessitated his exertion of intellect on minute distinctions. His admiration for the musical genius of Henry Purcell reflected not only his baroque taste but a certain Scotist quality: Scotus claimed that each body in nature had not merely a material form, but also a vital form—and from this Hopkins may have drawn a defense of his attraction to the superiority of motility, dappledness: "meaning motion fans fresh our wits with wonder."

Hopkins' metrical exactitude embodied his refusal, as a poet and as a Catholic, to omit complexity for the sake of ease. In writing "The Wreck of the Deutschland," he submitted his poetic subject to a formal plan that he had already more or less devised: "In the winter of '75," he wrote to Dixon, "I had long had haunting my ear the echo of a new rhythm which I now realised on paper. To speak shortly, it consists in scanning by accents or stresses along."[15] The result was a combination of sprung rhythm and counterpointed rhythm. He managed, furthermore, to tell the story of the shipwreck and deliver an unparalleled spiritual confession in an unfailingly perfect meter, which he claimed was "the rhythm of Greek tragic choruses or of Pindar."[16] One scholar remarked on the extraordinary accuracy of detail in Hopkins' effort:

> ". . . and so the sky keeps,
>   For the infinite air is unkind,
>   And the sea flint-flake, black-backed in the regular blow
>   Sitting Eastnortheast, in cursed quarter, the wind";

Few poets would find room in their metrical scheme for an expression such as "Sitting Eastnortheast"; the most accurate account of the wreck described the wind as "East-northeast," and Hopkins was not the man to falsify for the sake of a smooth metre.[17]

In baroque aesthetics, too, the reality of concrete particulars takes precedence over formal repose. The way Hopkins uses echoes, alliterations, and rhymes reproduces the multiplicity of separate identities that he detected in his subject, and the violent yoking of opposites ("lightning and love," "winter and warm," "Father and fondler of heart thou hast wrung")— a baroque technique—suggests the multiple, uncategorical nature of the divine. Yet he maintains coherence in spite of multiplicity. The chafing, unquiet rhythm of "The Windhover" reproduces the reality of balance amidst commotion, the motion against countermotion ending in equilibrium.

This liveliness, virtuosity, and sense of motion in Hopkins force the reader to participate actively in the experience of the poem. In baroque architecture, the profusion of porticoes, pilasters, columns, capitals, and so on, draws the viewer into an environment of quickened alternations; in baroque painting, optical illusions and extreme realism of portrayed experience bring the viewer into the world of the canvas, as though on a march from the Tiber to the door of St. Peter's, along a lengthy, decorated passage. The baroque challenge was how to make visible or sensible what was in fact abstract. In his anti-baroque Bible, Johann Joachim Winckelmann opposed the chaotic activity and splashes of paint of baroque art to the "noble simplicity and quiet grandeur" of the classics.

Chaotic activity, however, controlled by the strictest rhythmic plan, suited Hopkins' concept of the interaction of nature and supernature. The agony of opposition and invasion suffuses "The Wreck of the Deutschland." The first two lines of the poem,

> Thou mastering me
> God!

signal by means of a driving *tmesis* the invasion of daily life by divine Providence. The exactness and economy of that interruption—"God!"—separate the phrases "mastering me" and "Giver of breath and bread" the way lightning cleaves a tree. When Robert Bridges edited a selection of Hopkins for his anthology *The Spirit of Man*,[18] he tried to efface the signs of strain in that first stanza of "The Wreck":

> God mastering me;
> Giver of breath and bread;
> World's strand, sway of the sea;
> Lord of living and dead;
> Thou hast bound bones and veins in me, fasten'd me flesh
> And after at times almost unmade me with dread,
> Thy doing;

Compare this with Hopkins' original:

> THOU mastering me
> God! giver of breath and bread;
> World's strand, sway of the sea;
> Lord of living and dead;
> Thou hast bound bones and veins in me, fastened me flesh,

> And after it almost unmade, what with dread,
>   Thy doing:

Bridges seems to have had a vague sense of the contradictions and tension in the stanza, but none at all of how that tension was necessary to Hopkins' grasp of things. The strenuousness, the straining of flesh to become more than mere pagan fabric of flesh, is a true attribute of baroque, and of Hopkins. Beauty must be bought at great price, and the effort should show.

The Catholic tradition sees the Incarnation as a sanctification of this struggling flesh—which, like the senses and other faculties of humanity, must cooperate in praising God. We must give our best to God

> as, to the Infant Jesus, the shepherds presented lambs, and the kings, gold, frankincense, and myrrh. If the heavenly palaces unimaginably surpass all houses built by human hands, let men, at any rate, rear for God a cathedral to overtop their cottages; let all the arts enrich the sanctuary.[19]

The agitated sensuality of the baroque, in addition to disrupting the simplicity, repose, and quiet grandeur of the Renaissance, strove to transcend the limits of the material and of the sensual.

> The Baroque was the Catholic counterstatement to the reformers' attacks on the wealth of the Church and her use of painting and sculpture. Uncommited to any single style in architecture or the fine arts, the Church found in the Baroque appeal to the senses a mode compatible with her tradition.[20]

Iconoclastic movements have always viewed the seductions of the senses as the poisons of the soul. The baroque, in coincidence with the Catholic Reformation, made *use* of the senses to a spiritual end. St. Ignatius includes "Application of the Senses" as essential to *The Spiritual Exercises*. Here is the First Prelude of the First Exercise, Week One:

> This is a mental representation of the place. Attention must be called to the following point. When the contemplation or meditation is on something visible, for example, when we contemplate Christ our Lord, the representation will consist in seeing in the imagination the material place where the object is that we wish to contemplate. *I said material place* [italics mine], for example, the temple or the mountain where Jesus or His Mother is, according to the subject matter of the contemplation.[21]

The influence of this respect for the material is seen in Hopkins' poetic metaphors—though they may analogize immaterial concepts—they are more concrete, hard, and palpable. The effect of such a baroque aesthetic on poetry was "a strange tension between materiality and spirituality which almost defines the spirit of the Counter-Reformation; and from this attempt to prove to St. Thomas' fingers the substance of the insubstantial, baroque drawing and painting take their inception."[22]

To the medieval mind, each creature was a faithful representation, as though in a book or picture, of supernature. Consider this thirteenth-century lyric of Alain de Lille:

> *Omnis mundi creatura*
> *quasi liber et pictura*
> > *nobis est in speculum*
> *nostrae vitae, nostrae sortis,*
> *nostrae status, nostrae mortis,*
> > *fidele signaculum.*

> Every creature of the world
> as though a book and picture
> becomes to us a mirror

of our life, our fate
our condition, our death,
    faithfully represented.

The sixteenth and seventeenth centuries continued to use a medieval vocabulary in many ways, but the points of reference for their symbolism had changed. Eblem books—a sort of precursor of comic books with simple pictures accompanied by sententious mottoes and moral lessons—are the bridge between medieval and modern representations of reality. To generalize, medieval symbolism was so obvious, the immediate communication of its meaning so safely assumed, that moral messages could be simply *represented*. In a later age, when supernatural images were more distant from daily life, symbols had to be explained, couched in discussion. The great popularity of emblem books during the baroque period reveals an *esprit* of poetic discourse that represents and says at the same time, often to ridiculous effect. An example of an emblem with a moral message is an illustration of a man sitting in hell, with each of the seven deadly sins piercing him, each in the form of a sword, the point entering "the part of anatomy which is propense to a particular sin, each ending, beyond the hilt, in the head of a bird, beast or reptile to which the sin is natural—e.g., the goat for luxuria, for superbia the peacock."[23] The secret power of the Jesuits, who made great use of emblem books in their catechizing and evangelizing, seemed to reside in their grasp of how to direct the human senses to a spiritual end. Still, Protestants made use of this secret power, too. Quarles, the best-known Protestant emblematist poet, wrote in 1635: "Before the knowledge of letters God was knowne by hieroglyphicks. And, indeed, what are the Heavens, the earth, nay every Creature, but Hieroglyphicks and Emblemes of his Glory?"[24] A contemporary of Quarles, a Jesuit emblematist, wrote "Plotinus called the world the Poetry of God. I add, that this Poem is like a labrynth which is read in every direction, and gives intimation of, and points to, its Author."[25]

Through his grasp of transubstantiation and the sacramental presence of the divine in nature, Hopkins was able to dispense with drawings of hieroglyphs, emblems, and other obvious symbols of God's glory, for as the Jesuit emblematist, the world for Hopkins was "this Poem." He imitated nature in verse by effecting a pattern similar to the pattern of particulars in reality, which rhymed, repeated, alliterated, resonated. The pattern was often recondite in the poems on first reading. He wrote to Bridges about "The Wreck":

> Granted that it needs study and is obscure, for indeed I was not over-desirous that the meaning of all should be quite clear, at least unmistakeable, you might, without the effort that to make it all out would seem to have required, have nevertheless read it so that lines and stanzas should be left in the memory and superficial impressions deepened.[26]

Linguistically daring and formally conservative, Hopkins acted with maximum freedom within a very tight "rule." As W. H. Gardner said, "Far from being a mere 'metrical experiment,' the ode is unique in showing the maximum of rhythmic flexibility within a fixed stanzaic form."[27] Bridges, however, found the linguistic rebellion incompatible with formal conservatism, and argued to the poet that the obscurity of a poem such as "The Wreck" strained the reader. Strain, however, was something that Hopkins never cared to spare either himself or his audience, thinking—much like Ignatius in *The Spiritual Exercises*—that it would strengthen the vividness of sensation and inscape.

> When Bridges taxed him with obscurity, he kept insisting that he was clearing the ground for a new popular style.

The first essential was a return to strictness in the use of
words, and it is manifest to us today that his compact
method of joining them together compels them to be un-
derstood as he meant them to be, or understood not at
all.[28]

All of these qualities—metrical flourish, preference for
concrete particulars, repetition and ingenius rhyme, mixing
of opposites, mobility within a given space, crowding of im-
ages in a predetermined pattern to produce a particular
effect—are characteristic of the baroque manner. Hopkins
would not have imagined himself a metaphysical poet, mak-
ing use of the elaborate conceits and themes associated with
the seventeenth century (such as mutability, the brevity of
life, time, death, the dichotomy of spirit and flesh). Let us
consider, however, the following description of baroque po-
etry in Spain and Italy during the seventeenth century:

Baroque poets showed a decided preference in their im-
agery for . . . the concrete and specific, i.e., the particular
over the general (in contrast, for the most part, to Renais-
sance practice), often combining with the naturalistic.[29]

. . . excessively mannered, strained, often illogical, need-
lessly complex, and esoteric.[30]

Considering the Baroque "cult" of form and the esteem in
which it held inventiveness and novelty in art, one can
readily understand the temptation of poets to seek unusual
lexical items and bold, unexpected syntactical arrange-
ments.[31]

These are comments that could have been—and often were,
more or less—made about Hopkins. He was no stranger to
"unusual lexical items and bold, unexpected syntactical ar-
rangements," and even in theme produced some examples of

that metaphysical favorite, the *discordia concors* (reconciliation of opposites), as illustrated in such titles as "The Blessed Virgin Compared to the Air We Breathe" and "As Kingfishers Catch Fire."

Another theory of baroque sees it as a tendency to "materialize the spiritual," to infuse sacramental meaning into created nature. Critics of baroque art have often claimed that it failed in this goal, and that just the opposite effect was struck—that any spiritual content of an artistic expression became so burdened with the ornateness, complexity, and undeniable presence of the material that it lost its power to inspire. The light and ethereal qualities of the Gothic style were often thought to be superior. Yet the general disdain for baroque as "Mannerism" or "preciousness," decadence, mere sensuousness, and corruption, does not do justice to the potential of that style to breed inspired brilliance—as it does, I would argue, in Hopkins.

> We must not say that the corruption of metaphysical is the generation of baroque. . . . It is enough, perhaps, to remind ourselves that when we think of metaphysical, we do not think at once of St. Ignatius or Bernini or Marino, though we may do so a little later. We think first of a special moment in English poetry, a moment of plain but witty magniloquence, of a passionate poetry ballasted with learning and propelled by a sceptical ingenuity that may strike us as somehow very modern.[32]

Tridentine Catholicism took as its plastic and graphic expressions the churches of Rome, the paintings of Correggio, El Greco, and Rubens, the sculpture of Bernini, and the emblem books of the Jesuits. The Victorian Catholic revival provided material for the imagination of Pugin, Ruskin, and the Pre-Raphaelites. Baroque inventiveness was activated by images of angels and cherubs, the Sacred Heart, the ecstasies of the saints, and great martyrdoms; Victorians enjoyed a nostalgia for a romanticized version of the Middle Ages, as it might have been expressed in medieval decorative arts. Nowhere, however, in the age of the First Vatican Council does one find painting and architecture supervised by theologians, or religious orders founded to combat heresy, as one found in both the Gothic and baroque periods. Doubt and latitudinarianism in Victorian England had to be confronted by the individual; no central authority determined artistic goals; far from the medieval habit of preferring forgery, anonymity, and imitation to original personal expressions, the Victorian ideal of individualism called the artist to look into his *own* heart and write.

Why, in the midst of a nineteenth-century revival of "Catholic" tastes, should Hopkins have chosen a baroque manner over a Gothic one? The Gothick revival, the Cambridge-Camden Society, the Pre-Raphaelites—all looked to an age that was at once more spiritual and closer to nature than Erastian, industrial, Victorian England. These movements paralleled in the arts the efforts of the Tractarians and the later Anglo-Catholic reformers. In his admiration for the Rossettis and Ruskin, Hopkins became familiar with their program. An effort to spiritualize nature—while expressing itself in a style very different from the baroque—nevertheless reflects an interest common to all periods of Catholic reform in which a reassertion of the power of sacraments is foremost.

The Pre-Raphaelite brotherhood was founded by three gifted young painters, Dante Gabriel Rossetti, John Everett Millais, and William Holman Hunt. Dismissing the masters of the Royal Academy, they began by rejecting their generic conventions and academic manner of painting as superficial, stylized, and trivial. Instead, they took laborious measures to introduce sincerity, exactitude, and emotional engagement into their paintings. Their technique, which at first included painting with semitransparent colors over a wet white ground, "made for a luminous clarity perfectly suited to bring small details into prominence."[33] In science, philosophy, and now the arts, small details were brought more and more into prominence. This tendency reflected, among other things, an increasing respect for the status of concrete particulars. Transformed by sacramental belief, this view of "small details" could include a sanctification of reality instead of its reduction or degradation.

Yet just as the baroque manner digressed from its original spiritual ideal and became more purely decorative in the rococo, so also the Pre-Raphaelite ideal began to degenerate just as Hopkins was reaching his maturity. After 1868, " 'Pre-Raphaelitism' and 'Aestheticism' tend to become interchangeable terms to describe the Romantic medievalism of Rossetti and his circle; the original Pre-Raphaelite 'return to nature' in accordance with Ruskin's teaching is forgotten."[34] The Pre-Raphaelite effort to heal the rift between the material and the spiritual had certain things in common with Coleridge's desire for the imagination to spiritualize nature. It was Hopkins, however, who was able to go farthest with this ideal, because he made no recourse to sentimentality or to subjective concepts of nature. "It was Hopkins," wrote Humphry House, "not the aesthetes, who truly developed Pre-Raphaelite aims."[35] House claimed,

> One of the big problems for the Pre-Raphaelites and for all their generation was to try to see the daily life of Victorian England—complete with all its keepings of dress and furniture and social habits—as having an equivalent spiritual and human significance to that which medieval life had in all its details for medieval poets and painters. . . . [Patmore's] *The Angel in the House* is an attempt to invest an ordinary Victorian courtship and marriage in the prosperous educated classes with as deep a

spiritual and psychological significance as was felt to attach to the great loves of the past. . . . There seemed to be an irreparable cleavage between the facts of modern society and the depths it was recognised poetry ought to touch. This cleavage is not yet healed; all our living poets have been conscious of it; so were the Pre-Raphaelites.[36]

The direct use of a medium corresponded with a respect for natural fact in its actual state rather than with that taste for imprecise emotion excited by imprecise observations associated with Romanticism and nonreligious symbolism. Ruskin's *Modern Painters* was published and met with much debate. The critic for the *Westminster Review* was George Eliot, and she approved, in her *belles-lettres* articles, of Ruskin's positions: "The truth of infinite value that he teaches is *realism*—the doctrine that all truth and beauty are to be attained by a humble and faithful study of nature, and not by substituting vague forms, bred by imagination on the mists of feeling, in place of definite, substantive reality."[37] That Hopkins studied and admired Ruskin is well-known from his letters, notebooks, and sketches, and Ruskin influenced not only his approach to nature but the proper way to describe it. Radicalness and extroversion of language were Hopkins' conscious effort to counteract "Parnassian" poetic diction. His use of language reflects a direct experience of God. As the baroque tried to infuse the material world with a spiritual meaning which it had lately begun to lose, as the Pre-Raphaelites tried to reproduce a "medieval" significance in Victorian life, so Hopkins localized in language a kind of power that had grown subjective and diffuse. What George Eliot perceived in Ruskin as *realism* took form for Hopkins in the objective dogmas of sacramental theology. And just as a sacrament must be recognizable in its particular setting, Hopkins required that his message be placed in an unmistakable, visible, technical order.

The efforts of the Counter-Reformation baroque to re-establish "medieval" beliefs were not entirely successful, and many critics have disparaged the types of baroque poetry as a reflection of the strain, excess, and relative failure of the period. J. Hillis Miller has called baroque language "empty" and "visibly disintegrating." The intensity and rapid movement of baroque poetic structure reflect a losing battle to regain that lost spiritual meaning, calmly possessed by an earlier, religiously uniform age, when

> The Eucharist was the archetype of the divine analogy whereby created things participated in the supernatural reality they signified. . . . The symbols and metaphors of poetry . . . were borrowed from the divine analogies of nature. Poetry was meaningful in the same way as nature itself—by a communion of the verbal symbols with the reality they named.[38]

> The old symbolism of analogical participation is gradually replaced by the modern poetic symbolism of reference at a distance. Like the Zwinglian Eucharist such symbols designate an absence, not a presence.[39]

According to Miller, as sacraments and language—the symbols joining a fallen world with a distant God—lost their power, and the arts became more mobile, twisting, compounded of metaphors and motifs in their search for meaning, and more decorative in their superficial efforts to cover the absence:

> Baroque poetry represents a violent effort by the human imagination to keep open the avenues of communication between man and God. It tries to express, in a language which is visibly disintegrating and becoming empty, a divine reality which is in the very act of disappearing from the world. . . . But the God wthin nature and the God beyond nature gradually separate from one another. . . . Baroque art is the expression of the movement of this sep-

aration, just as, in nineteenth-century England, Evangel-
icalism and the Catholic revival are belated attempts to
stop the "melancholy, long, withdrawing roar" of the sea
of faith.[40]

Hopkins' response to the absence of God in the world
was to find in the Roman Catholic doctrine of transubstan-
tiation a relief from the "sordidness" of life. As a Jesuit he
sought God through discipline and action. Discussing one of
his most baroque poems, "The Leaden Echo and the Golden
Echo," he wrote to Bridges:

> You must know that words like *charm* and *enchantment*
> will not do: the thought is of beauty as of something that
> can be physically kept and lost and *by physical things
> only*. . . . You will see that this limits the choice of words
> very much indeed. . . . *Back* is not pretty, but it gives
> that feeling of *physical constraint* which I want.[41] [Third
> and fifth italics mine.]

The images of wretchedness, wrestling, and struggle in the
last poems of Hopkins' life suggest not an absence of God,
but an engagement of two wills. The dialectical structure of
many or most of Hopkins' poems can be seen as either me-
dieval or baroque; it also reflects his perception of *otherness
present* in the world. The premise of Miller's argument is
that "Post-medieval literature records . . . the gradual with-
drawal of God from the world."[42] It seems possible for Mil-
ler that God has actually, literally withdrawn. Although Mil-
ler's discussion is characteristically intelligent and assiduously
documented by examples from literature, it is too easy to as-
sume that industry and cities make God inaccessible. This
contrast of the happy Middle Ages with miserable moder-
nity, with the baroque artist existing, transitionally, in a pe-
riod of unsuccessful struggle, overlooks the possibility of an
imminent God present in history.

It is likely that spiritual poverty and doubt flourish more

in a society where there is no commonly recognized system of symbols binding the human and the divine. But Hopkins himself searched for the offer of divine presence, in the form of the Catholic sacraments, and accepted it. Rather than limiting his religious understanding to the lessons of private experience, a kind of spiritual positivism of the nineteenth century, he located God in the objective details of the Incarnation and sacramental elements. The "perspectivism" that turned God and his angels into reality, if someone still believed in them, found no place in Hopkins. Yet the relative solitude of his position in late Victorian Protestantism, as well as his membership in the sixteenth-century foundation of the Society of Jesus, made his (perhaps unconscious) embrace of a baroque manner seem especially appropriate. Far from "empty" and "visibly disintegrating," Hopkins' language against the background of other Victorian poetry was full of vitality, substance, and objective meaning.

Many of Hopkins' poems reveal baroque sensibility: "The Wreck of the Deutschland" in its grandeur, monumentality, and compression; "Pied Beauty" in its preference for irregularity; "The Leaden Echo and the Golden Echo" for its use of dialectic and repetition; "Spelt from Sibyl's Leaves" in its contorted, compact multiplicity of movements. In "To What Serves Mortal Beauty," Hopkins tells us that our response to beauty should be to "Merely meet it; own / Home at heart, heaven's sweet gift; I then leave, let that alone." Inscape and detachment: things tell of their Creator, and enjoy no selfishness, and thus lead to grace. He refers to "Purcell tune" for the poem's first example of mortal beauty and says, "See: it does this: keeps warm / Men's wits to the things that are." This is George Eliot's realism, *the things that are.*

Purcell was a baroque composer and Hopkins' favorite. Just as the sonnet which bears the name of Scotus trips lightly over the character it names, as though the human vehicle for Hopkins' insights into divine truth were secondary,

the sonnet which bears the name of Purcell actually cele-
brates Purcell's lack of self-consciousness. It is such a diffi-
cult sonnet that Hopkins continued to explain it to Bridges
in letters for many years. Even when he wrote the poem, he
preceded it with an explanatory prose epigraph: "The poet
wishes well to the divine genius of Purcell and praises him
that, whereas other musicians have given utterance to the
moods of man's mind, he has, beyond that, uttered in notes
the very make and species of man as created both in him
and in all men generally." "The very make and species . . .
in all men generally" is parallel to the idea that Duns Scotus
is a rare-veined unraveller of general reality. Both Scotus
and Purcell express something universal as well as something
unique. The greatest genius, "divine genius," comes closest
to the image of God, and thus to universal human nature. It
was simplicity, not originality, that Hopkins most admired,
and the unselfconscious "make" of people rather than indi-
vidual idiosyncrasy.

Demonstration, not argumentation or disputation, con-
sumed Hopkins' poetic energy. It was as though words them-
selves represented a struggle, as though Hopkins was always
seeking to make a thing exist in a poem as it does in nature.
Harmony for Hopkins was experienced as simplicity: "Noth-
ing is so pregnant and straightforward to the truth as simple
yes and *is*."[43] But this harmony could exist only after a mani-
festation of particularity had been perceived, understood,
and affirmed. The sestet of the sonnet "Henry Purcell" is
an example of this admiration for the capacity of music to
manifest rather than discuss, and poetic imitation of it. Here
is the entire sonnet:

Have fair fallen, O fair, fair have fallen, so dear
To me, so arch-especial a spirit as heaves in Henry Purcell,
An age is now since passed, since parted; with the reversal
Of the outward sentence low lays him, listed to a heresy, here.

Not mood in him nor meaning, proud fire or sacred fear,
Or love or pity or all that sweet notes not his might nursle:
It is the forgèd feature finds me; it is the rehearsal
Of own, of abrúpt sélf there so thrusts on, so throngs the ear.

Let him oh! with his air of angels then lift me, lay me! only I'll
Have an eye to the sakes of him, quaint moonmarks, to his pelted
     plumage under
Wings: so some great stormfowl, whenever he has walked his
     while

The thunder-purple seabeach plumèd purple-of-thunder,
If a wuthering of his palmy snow-pinions scatter a colossal smile
Off him, but meaning motion fans fresh our wits with wonder.

In the first quatrain, Hopkins hopes that Purcell has been
forgiven for being a Protestant,[44] and that something fair has
befallen him because he is "so dear / To me." The rhythm in
the poem, like that of Purcell's music, is contrapuntal, a
stretching of the distance between stress and pitch. The stress
gradually goes from soft to hard in the sestet; the breathy,
lulling series of words with open vowels and ells—"Oh!" . . .
air . . . angels . . . lift . . . lay . . . only I'll"—moves to
the stark Anglo-Saxon "sakes of him, quaint moonmarks, to
his pelted plumage," and then to the majestic "walked his
while / . . . thunder purple . . . purple-of-thunder," ending
with the compressed, alliterative, hard-stressed "meaning mo-
tion fans fresh our wits with wonder." "Meaning motion" is
a phrase he invents to imply that in action things express
their purpose, and our "wits" (the second time he uses this
seventeenth-century word in connection with Purcell) are
fanned fresh by it. Motion is not simply part of the baroque
manner; it is the antidote to entropy, to eternal death:

A coil or spiral is then a type of the Devil, who is called
the old (or original) serpent, and this I suppose because

of its "swale" or subtle and imperceptible drawing in to-
wards its head or centre, and it is a type of death, of mo-
tion lessening and at last ceasing. . . . God gave things a
forward and perpetual motion.[45]

Hopkins wrote his first letter of explanation about this
poem to Bridges about a month after he sent the sonnet, in
the spring of 1876, saying, "The sestet . . . is not so clearly
worked out as I could wish:

> The thought is that as the seabird opening its wings with
> a whiff of wind in your face means the whirr of the mo-
> tion, but also unaware gives you a whiff of knowledge
> about his plumage, the marking of which stamps his spe-
> cies, that he does not mean, so Purcell, seemingly intent
> only on the thought or feeling he is to express or call out,
> incidentally lets you remark the individualising marks of
> his own genius.[46]

Hopkins' feelings about genius here echo his remarks to
Dixon on the balance of his two vocations. When a thing
is doing or being the self that God created it to do or be,
when it is most distinctively determined, and the exercise of
its genius is remarked *incidentally,* then it is most perfectly
at ease and at one with God's will; its genius is entirely di-
vine. This is not so much a self-negating statement of humil-
ity as it is a theological reflection on several Christian ideas,
most certainly on the "First Principle and Foundation" of *The
Spiritual Exercises* (beginning, "Man was created to praise").
Genius must be expressed only incidentally to what you
are doing intently, in the praise and service of your Cre-
ator, who alone determines the distinctiveness of your
being.

For Hopkins, the joy of knowledge and the pleasure one
takes in explicit personality belong to the observer. "It is the
forgèd feature finds me; it is the rehearsal / Of own, of abrúpt

sélf." Hopkins adores the distinctiveness of Purcell with his arch-especial spirit. The particularity of a creature, of a poetic subject, is fully expressed here—though what Hopkins praises most in him is that this particularity seems to escape his notice.

There is of course danger, or at least risk, in equating rhetorical with literary-historical phenomena, or especially with spiritual ones. So what might be useful in identifying Hopkins' habits as baroque must withstand the criticism that they are equally Victorian, or Mannerist, or Scotist, or Pre-Raphaelite—and neither of these is quite true. Whichever style he may participate in from time to time must be recognized as tangential to and essentially separate from the individual, private, and in each consecutive example of it, unique experience of writing a poem. The way he values and perceives particulars may be called sacramental, the language he uses to describe them, baroque—but only Hopkins' "own, abrupt self" can liberate the self of each thing perceived and allow "outflow."

Coleridge's sacramental view—in which accident is to substance as symbol is to the thing symbolized—contributes a nineteenth-century gloss to the innate assumption of simultaneity and irreducibility in the orthodox Catholic sacrament, and Hopkins is heir to both traditions. In Hopkins, the sacramental view included an original theology of the particular: a perfect perception of the *other* heightened the identity of the self; on apprehension of its separate identity, a recognition of one's own radical self would follow. The "fiduciary" element in this doctrine of perception includes the trust that, when touched in its bower of bone, the heart will rise to the difficulty, dazzling but obscure, of perceiving the active presence of God in things. The use of language within this doctrine is interpersonal, associative, revelatory—

language becomes the incarnation of certain truths about God. The Incarnation of Christ was the action of a transcendent being made *particular*. Hopkins' theory of the particular is often identified as Scotus' *haecceitas,* his "infinite individuality," his "thisness" which connects to God.

The most perceptibly identified and particularized things in creation, those things whose individuality is most clearly related to the infinite, are those in which nature and action are simultaneous or identical. Identity thus resides in the resilience between the finite and infinite, between stillness and motion, and the most resilient are such things as fire, tolling bells, and things which fluctuate, rhyme, or fly. The end of Hopkins' effort in each poem is to discard neutral or unstressed elements and to reside in what is most individuated, most perfectly itself. The resilience of things is detected at moments when they are drawn to each other according to their similarities and their mobility. Thus they must grapple for individual survival: the heart in hiding stirs for the falcon, drawn to the dappled dawn; and the wretch, exemplary in resilience, grapples with God.

Conclusion

During an age which witnessed the growth of the science of linguistics, in a time and place which knew a religion largely divested of sacramental power, the Victorian Jesuit Gerard Manley Hopkins found in the Catholic faith and released in his poetry the tremendous power at the heart of human language. His vocation as a Jesuit gave him his essential vocabulary as a poet. And these two vocations—priest and poet—may well have been in some degree of conflict throughout most of his short career, though there seems to be a moral miracle in his last poems. These are often called "the terrible sonnets." The spiritual struggle, which began with the first lines he wrote as a priest—"Thou mastering me / God!"—ends with the breaking of his scruples and the subjugation of his will. The victory is won through desolation and death to the ways of the will, to "these last strands of man / In me," "selfwrung, selfstrung." The opponent against whom he has been wrestling is "(my God!) my God." In the end, through a convening of the two vocations, Hopkins achieved the condition of "immortal diamond," of resurrection.

His belief in the transubstantiation of the Eucharist gave him the synthesizing power that Coleridge had received from poetic imagination. In Hopkins' sacramentalized landscape, both physical and metaphysical, energy was entering a closed system every time bread and wine were consecrated, and thus raised to a higher level of energy. This was the *opposite* of entropy and dissociation. His poetic diction showed signs of that infused, endless energy, which could force language to its limits. The Incarnation—which is the original *type* of a sacrament, of the Divine entering material nature—is reenacted in transubstantiated bread and wine. The Incarnation also raises the question of how an individual relates to the universal. Hopkins' concern with the relationship of the particular to the whole, and with the human capacity to intuit or instress it, was the basic question behind not only his *ars poetica* but his spirituality. Individuals, no matter how odd or how opposite, are related to one another through human intuition and through their relationship to the whole, to God. Hopkins transcended Victorian positivism, subjectivism, and theories of individual isolation by means of his absorption of Duns Scotus' *haecceitas*, or infinite individuality.

Finally, his attention to particulars, his preference for distinctiveness, and the compressed mobility of his language identify Hopkins with a baroque aesthetic. His status as a Jesuit in a Protestant and even actively anti-Catholic milieu identifies him with a baroque spiritual tradition. His rhetoric is at once Anglo-Saxonate and baroque, and in this he is utterly original, the "immortal diamond" of his own poetry.

Notes

INTRODUCTION

1. F. R. Leavis, *New Bearings in English Poetry* (first edition, London, 1932; Penguin reprint, 1982), p. 119.
2. C. C. Abbott, ed., *The Letters of Gerard Manley Hopkins to Robert Bridges* (Oxford, 1935), p. 180. Henceforth, *L* I.
3. *L* I, 265.
4. Margaret Bottrall, ed., *Gerard Manley Hopkins: Poems, A Casebook* (London, 1975), p. 60.
5. Donald E. Stanford, ed., *The Selected Letters of Robert Bridges*, two volumes (London, 1983, 1984).
6. Ibid., I, 204.
7. P. N. Furbank, *Times Literary Supplement*, 1 Feb. 1985, p. 107.
8. Stanford, I, 204.
9. Indeed it has been argued by Tom Dunne in *Gerard Manley Hopkins: A Comprehensive Bibliography* (London, 1976), p. xviii.
10. Robert Bridges, dedicatory sonnet to the first edition of Hopkins' *Poems* (Oxford, 1918).
11. W. H. Gardner, *Gerard Manley Hopkins: A Study of Poetic Idiosyncrasy in Relation to Poetic Tradition* (London, 1949), II, 8.

12. Humphry House and Graham Storey, eds., *The Journals and Papers of Gerard Manley Hopkins* (Oxford, 1959), p. 71. Henceforth, *JP*.

13. Ibid.

14. Donald McChesney, *A Hopkins Commentary* (London, 1968), p. 5.

15. The length of his period of silence is usually reported as seven years, though G.M.H. himself says ten years: "the Bremen stanza, which was, I think, the first written after ten years' interval of silence" (*L* I, 44).

16. *JP*, p. 230.

17. *L* I, 66.

18. *L* I, 190.

19. Stanford, I, 31.

20. Donald McChesney offers a dissenting report that the first printing produced two thousand copies, *A Hopkins Commentary*, p. 4.

21. They include John Pick's *G.M.H.: Priest and Poet* (London, 1942), which was the first to imply that Hopkins' two vocations were inseparable and mutual; E. E. Phare's *The Poetry of G.M.H.* (Cambridge, 1933, which was expressly non-Catholic and even anti-Catholic); and Fr. Gerald Lahey's *G.M.H.* (London, 1930), which simplifies Hopkins' life into a type of Jesuit hagiography. Also published in the 1940s were W. H. Gardner's magisterial two volume *G.M.H.: A Study of Poetic Idiosyncrasy in Relation to Poetic Tradition* (London, 1949); *Immortal Diamond*, essays by members of the Society of Jesus (New York, 1941); and *G.M.H.* (London, 1949), essays by the Kenyon critics.

22. Dunne, *Bibliography* (London, 1976).

23. Bernard Bergonzi, *G.M.H.* (New York, 1977); and Paddy Kitchen, *G.M.H.* (New York, 1979).

24. Ms. Kitchen in particular seeks to uncover information that might make the reading of Hopkins' life more salacious. The Society of Jesus gave her access to his unpublished confessional notes, and in "a breach of courtesy to the copyright holders," to which she admits, she uses these to dwell on the dubious topic of Hopkins' possible but unexpressed sexual inclinations.

25. C. C. Abbott, ed., *Further Letters of Gerald Manley Hopkins* (London, 1938), p. 249. Henceforth, *L* III.
26. Quoted in G. F. Lahey, S.J., *G.M.H.* (London, 1930), p. 33.
27. This correspondence has been analyzed in two essays by Humphry House, *All in Due Time: The Collected Essays and Broadcast Talks* (London, 1955).
28. Philip Endean, S.J., "The Spirituality of G.M.H.," *The Hopkins Quarterly,* VIII, 3, 126.
29. An essay by Krystyna Kapitulka, *Structural Principles of G.M.H.'s Poetry* (Warsaw, 1976) compares Hopkins' poetic system with the theories of the Polish avant-garde critics, especially Jan Mukarovsky, whose concepts of "foregrounding" and "underthought" emphasize the conscious devices, the "non-automatic" aspects of poetic composition. This strikes me as another and rather strained way of describing Mannerism, a habit that paralleled Hopkins' practice in certain ways.
30. Michael Sprinker, *"A Counterpoint of Dissonance":* *The Aesthetics and Poetry of Gerard Manley Hopkins* (Baltimore, 1980), provides an interesting study analyzing Hopkins' poetry as occurring within a "pattern" of other "lingual events," especially those of Mallarmé.

CHAPTER ONE

1. W. H. Gardner, *Gerard Manley Hopkins: A Study of Poetic Idiosyncrasy in Relation to Poetic Tradition* (London, 1949), I, 2.
2. Ibid.
3. Humphry House, "A Note on Hopkins' Religious Life," *New Verse,* No. 14 (April 1935), 3. Quoted in Gardner, I, 3.
4. C. C. Abbott, ed., *The Correspondence of Gerard Manley Hopkins and Richard Watson Dixon* (Oxford, 1935), p. 150. Henceforth, *L* II.
5. L. L. Martz, *The Poetry of Meditation* (New Haven, Conn., 1954).

6. Louis J. Puhl, S.J., *The Spiritual Exercises of St. Ignatius* (Chicago, 1951), pp. 52–53.

7. John Wain, "An Idiom of Desperation," Chatterton Lecture on an English Poet, British Academy Pamphlet, Proceedings of the British Academy XLV (1959), 187.

8. *L* I, 304.

9. *JP*, p. 84. Hopkins has referred to this previously as "Parnassian," which he defines as a kind of poetic language which "can be written without inspiration . . . common in professedly descriptive pieces," *JP*, p. 38.

10. F. R. Leavis, *New Bearings in English Poetry* (London, 1932), p. 164.

11. *L* I, 46.

12. Ibid., 303. Hopkins is referring to his sonnet "Thou Art Indeed Just, Lord."

13. Leavis, pp. 164–65.

14. *L* I, 66.

15. Ibid., 46.

16. Ibid.

17. *L* III, 17.

18. *L* I, 47.

19. Kathleen Raine, "Hopkins—Nature and Supernature," *Third Annual Lecture*, The Hopkins Society (1972), p. 2.

20. J. Hillis Miller, *The Linguistic Moment* (Princeton, N.J., 1985), p. 265.

21. *L* II, 94.

22. Ibid., 137–38.

23. See Jean-Georges Ritz, *Robert Bridges and Gerard Manley Hopkins, A Literary Friendship* (London, 1960).

24. *L* I, 275.

25. Ibid., 46.

26. Humphry House, ed., *Notebooks and Papers* (Oxford, 1937), p. 416n.

27. *L* I, 42–43.

28. Ibid., 41.

29. Ibid., 44.

30. *L* II, 93–94.

31. Ibid., 95.

32. Christopher Devlin, S.J., ed., *The Sermons and Devotional Writings of Gerard Manley Hopkins* (Oxford, 1959), p. 215. Henceforth, *SDW*.

33. Endean, 109.

34. Humphry House, *All in Due Time*, p. 170.

35. *L* III, 256.

36. *L* I, 24.

37. *L* I, 66.

38. *L* II, 14.

39. *L* I, 174–75.

40. Philip Endean, S.J., "The Spirituality of G.M.H.," *HQ*, VIII, 3, 125.

41. Puhl, *The Spiritual Exercises*, p. 75.

42. *L* II, 88.

43. *L* II, 89–90.

44. Ibid., 93.

45. Ibid., 88.

46. Bernadette Ward, "Poet and Priest in the Terrible Sonnets: Gerard Manley Hopkins," Senior Honors Thesis, Harvard University, 1981.

47. *L* I, 126.

48. Puhl, *The Spiritual Exercises*, p. 157.

49. Ibid., p. 155.

50. Ibid., p. 142.

51. Ward, p. 21.

52. Endean, 116.

53. *SDW*, p. 262.

54. *L* I, 270.

55. Apparently there followed an unpleasant exchange concerning the sonnet, to which Bridges referred in a later letter to Canon Dixon: "I have not been able to write you a letter about Gerard. . . . You will however like to see his last letters and verses. The last letter he wrote me I have, but very strangely it happened that the only two letters of his which I ever destroyed were the two which he wrote me preceding that. . . . It was very like a sort of quarrel. . . . The letters were rather bitter, and I put them in the fire." Stanford, *Selected Letters of RB*, I, 188.

56. Ibid., I, 186.

57. Bridges, who was a medical doctor, wrote to Hopkins' mother after his death: "I always considered that he was over nervous about himself and exaggerated his symptoms." Stanford, I, 201.

CHAPTER TWO

1. This designation is used by John Coulson in *Newman and the Common Tradition* (London, 1970), pp. 3–4.

2. In *Poetry and Dogma* (Rutgers, 1954).

3. This term is used by Coulson.

4. Coulson, p. 4.

5. Respectively, Wordsworth ("The Prelude"), Shakespeare (Sonnet 146), Hopkins (Sonnet 44), Luke 22:19 (cf. Matthew 26:26 and Mark 14:22).

6. W. K. Wimsatt, *The Verbal Icon* (University of Kentucky Press, 1954), p. 268.

7. Coulson, p. 4.

8. Emerson R. Marks, *Coleridge on the Language of Verse* (Princeton, N.J., 1981), p. 15.

9. *Victorian Devotional Poetry: The Tractarian Mode* (Cambridge, Mass., 1981), pp. 18–19.

10. Ibid., p. 19. It is the *primary imagination* that is a repetition in the finite mind of the eternal act of creation in the infinite I AM. The poetic imagination is an "echo" of this primary imagination.

11. Bishop Butler's *Analogy* was a favorite of Coleridge's. In 1736, Bishop Butler argued in this work against the Deists that revealed religion conforms with what is observable in nature.

12. J. Robert Barth, S.J., *Coleridge and Christian Doctrine* (Cambridge, Mass., 1969), pp. 168–69.

13. *The Book of Common Prayer* (Greenwich, Conn., 1953), p. 607.

14. Barth, p. 171.

15. Quoted by Coulson, p. 3.

16. At the Fourth Lateran Council in 1215, transubstan-

tiation was declared to be the "authentic teaching" of the Church.

17. Philip Edgcumbe Hughes, *Theology of the English Reformation* (Grand Rapids, Mich., 1965), pp. 189–222; C. W. Dugmore, *The Mass and the English Reformers* (London, 1958), pp. 23–80.

18. *L* III, 17.

19. Ibid., 79.

20. James V. Baker, *The Sacred River: Coleridge's Theory of the Imagination* (Louisiana State University Press, 1957), see especially pp. 210–11.

21. Cited by J. Robert Barth, *The Symbolic Imagination: Coleridge and the Romantic Tradition* (Princeton, N.J., 1977).

22. Walter Jackson Bate, ed., *Criticism: The Major Texts* (New York, 1952), p. 362.

23. Miller, *The Linguistic Moment*, p. 232.

24. Ibid., p. 231.

25. Ibid., p. 233.

26. Walter Pater, *The Renaissance* (New York, 1959; originally published, 1873), p. 95.

27. Miller, *The Linguistic Moment*, p. 246.

28. Irving Massey, *The Uncreating Word* (Bloomington, Ind., 1980), p. 93.

29. *L* I, 169.

30. In *Poetry and Dogma* (Rutgers, 1954).

31. Ibid., p. 56.

32. J. Hillis Miller, *The Disappearance of God* (Cambridge, Mass., 1975), p. 3.

33. House, *All in Due Time*, p. 157.

34. James Leggio, "The Science of a Sacrament," *The Hopkins Quarterly*, IV, 2, 63.

35. Ibid., 64.

36. McChesney, *A Hopkins Commentary*, p. 29.

37. "Parnassian" is what Hopkins defined as passable but uninspired poetic diction, *JP*, p. 38.

38. *L* I, 89.

39. James Milroy, *The Language of Gerard Manley Hopkins* (London, 1978), p. 117.

40. *L* I, 89.

41. These examples are provided by Paul L. Mariani in *A Commentary on the Complete Poems of Gerard Manley Hopkins* (Ithaca, N.Y., 1970), pp. 86–87.

42. *L* I, 44–45. To the questioned term "molossic," the editor notes, "No: amphibrachic."

43. *JP*, p. 12.

44. Herbert Read, *English Prose Style* (New York, 1952), pp. 5–6.

45. Ibid., p. 6.

46. Louis Rader discusses the connection in "Romantic Structure and Theme in Hopkins' Poetry," *The Hopkins Quarterly*, I, 2, 93–107.

47. Kathleen Raine, "Hopkins—Nature and Supernature," *Third Annual Lecture*, The Hopkins Society (1972), p. 2.

48. *L* I, 163; he confesses, "I was fascinated with *cynghanedd* or consonant-chime, and, as in Welsh *englyns*, 'the sense,' as one of themselves said, 'gets the worst of it.' "

49. Mariani in *A Commentary on the Complete Poems of Gerard Manley Hopkins* points out that this series of fragmentary details is an "interlocking pattern of assimilative consonants chiming down the alphabetical scale. . . . Everything in nature, for all its quaint distinctiveness, forms part of a larger pattern. It is a good example of Hopkins' delightful yet serious wordplaying" (p. 100).

50. Excerpts from Coleridge's notebooks are quoted in Patricia M. Ball, *The Science of Aspects* (London, 1971). This passage, p. 24.

51. *JP*, pp. 136–37.

52. Ball, p. 27.

53. *JP*, p. 196.

54. *JP*, p. 185.

55. *JP*, p. 207.

56. Except that he refers at one point to the sun as "Swimming—like looking down into a boiling pot or a swinging pail, or into a bowl of quicksilver shaken"; this letter appears as an appendix entitled "An Uncollected Letter from Hopkins to Nature, 30 October 1884," in Ball pp. 148–50.

57. Ball, pp. 8–9.
58. Ibid., p. 105.

CHAPTER THREE

1. Briefly, that all living things evolved from a few simple forms of life, which were modified and adapted according to a principle of survival of the fittest. Darwin's findings as a naturalist contradicted not only a literal reading of the biblical account of the origin of life but, to many minds, the notion of a divinely ordained natural order.
2. Geoffrey Grigson, "A Passionate Science," reprinted in Bottrall, *Gerard Manley Hopkins: Poems, A Casebook,* p. 153.
3. Raine, "Hopkins–Nature and Supernature," pp. 4–5.
4. The influence that Darwin, like Coleridge, had on Hopkins is one that I assume. Darwin's theories, like those of Coleridge, had tremendous impact on the intellectual climate and movements of the nineteenth century. Hopkins mentions "Darwinism" a couple of times in his letters and notebooks, and although he does not address Darwinian theories formally, he was aware of them and their implications.
5. Ball, *The Science of Aspects,* p. 3.
6. I. 1498, quoted in Ball, p. 18.
7. Ibid., p. 18.
8. *L* III, 92.
9. *L* III, 19.
10. *JP,* p. 221.
11. *L* I, 169.
12. *L* I, 221.
13. Christopher Devlin, S.J., *The Psychology of Duns Scotus* (Oxford, 1950), p. 16.
14. *SDW,* p. 195.
15. *JP,* p. 125.
16. Raine, "Hopkins–Nature and Supernature," p. 3.
17. *SDW,* p. 102.
18. *JP,* p. 125.

19. Ibid., p. 125.

20. *L* III, 222.

21. This is the logical extension of a "fiduciary" view of language. It was Bridges' misunderstanding of the degree to which Hopkins took this that led, in part, to his criticism of Hopkins' lack of poetic decorum.

22. E. R. August, *Word Inscapes: A Study of the Poetic Vocabulary of Gerard Manley Hopkins* (Ph.D. Diss., Pittsburgh, 1964), p. 50.

23. *JP*, pp. 101–2.

24. *SDW*, p. 123.

25. *JP*, p. 120.

26. *SDW*, pp. 124–25.

27. Carol T. Christ, *The Finer Optic* (New Haven, Conn., 1974), p. 166.

28. *JP*, p. 127.

29. Ibid.

30. Raine, "Hopkins—Nature and Supernature," pp. 9–10.

31. *SDW*, pp. 124–25.

32. Ibid., pp. 338–39, Appendix II.

33. Ibid., p. 151.

34. Ibid., p. 123.

35. James Finn Cotter, *Inscape* (Pittsburgh, 1972), p. 14.

36. Geoffrey Hartman, *The Unmediated Vision* (New Haven, Conn., 1954), p. 122.

37. *JP*, p. 269.

38. Bottrall, *A Casebook*, p. 113, quoting from Christopher Devlin, S.J., "Hopkins and Duns Scotus," *New Verse* (April 1935).

39. *JP*, p. 25.

40. Ibid., p. 24.

41. Ibid., p. 66.

42. Ibid., p. 243.

43. Ibid., p. 195.

44. *L* I, 66.

45. Donald Davie, *Purity of Diction in English Verse* (London, 1967), p. 182.

46. *SDW*, p. 29.
47. Ibid., p. 123.
48. *L* I, 291.
49. *SDW*, p. 123.
50. Ibid., p. 45.

CHAPTER FOUR

1. In *Renaissance und Barock* (Munich, 1888).
2. Heinrich Wölfflin, *Renaissance and Baroque*, trans. by Kathrin Simon (Ithaca, N.Y., 1966), p. 15.
3. Harold B. Segel, *The Baroque Poem* (New York, 1974), p. 15.
4. René Wellek, *Concepts of Criticism* (New Haven, Conn., 1963), p. 70.
5. More recent scholars have preferred to call it "Catholic Reformation," thus reducing the implication that it was simply a negative reaction instead of a positive action.
6. Wölfflin, *Renaissance and Baroque*, p. 92.
7. Wellek, p. 92.
8. Ibid., p. 103.
9. Ibid., p. 108. A good review of the relationship between baroque art and the Jesuits can be found in Rudolph Wittkower and Irma B. Jaffe, eds., *Baroque Art: The Jesuit Contribution* (New York, 1972).
10. E. R. Norman, *Anti-Catholicism in Victorian England* (New York, 1968), p. 20.
11. Ibid., p. 13.
12. *JP*, p. 289.
13. Author's Preface, W. H. Gardner, *The Complete Poems of Gerard Manley Hopkins* (fourth edition, Oxford, 1967), p. 45.
14. F. O. Mathiessen, *American Renaissance* (Oxford, 1966), p. 587.
15. *L* II, 14.
16. *L* I, 157.

17. Milroy, *The Language of GMH*, p. 120.

18. Robert Bridges, *The Spirit of Man* (London, 1916), p. 53.

19. Austin Warren, *Richard Crashaw: A Study in Baroque Sensibility* (Baton Rouge, La., 1939), p. 67.

20. Ibid., p. 66.

21. Puhl, *The Spiritual Exercises of St. Ignatius*, p. 25. Joseph A. Devenny, S.J., contributes the following comment:

> The Ignatian term "application of the senses" is *technical*, referring to a specific type of prayer, e.g. the application of the senses in the exercise on Hell, or the application of the senses in the second week to the mysteries of the Incarnation and the Nativity (121–26). The passage quoted is 47 which is the sole description of what is called "a composition of place." It of course appeals to the imagination. . . . The text of 124 in Corbishley's translation calls for the quite unusual: "Smell the indescribable fragrance and taste the boundless sweetness of the divinity. Apply the same senses (i.e. vision, hearing, smell, taste—but not touch) to the virtues and other qualities of the soul, in different degrees."

22. Warren, *Richard Crashaw*, p. 74.

23. Ibid., p. 69; from Füllöp-Miller, *The Secret Power of the Jesuits*.

24. Quoted in Rosemary Freeman, *English Emblem Books* (London, 1948), p. 41.

25. Quoted in Mario Praz, *Studies in Seventeenth-Century Imagery* (London and New York, 1939), p. 17.

26. *L* I, 50.

27. Gardner, *Poems*, fourth edition, p. xxiii.

28. Robert Graves and Laura Riding, *A Survey of Modernist Poetry* (London, 1928), p. 90.

29. Segel, *The Baroque Poem*, p. 115.

30. Ibid., p. 104.

31. Ibid., p. 103.

32. Frank Kermode, ed., *The Metaphysical Poets* (New York, 1969), p. 32.

33. James Sambrook, ed., *Pre-Raphaelitism* (University of Chicago Press, 1974), p. 1.

34. Sambrook, p. 8.

35. IIouse, *All in Due Time*, p. 157.

36. Ibid., pp. 153–54.

37. Westminster Review, LXV (April 1856), 626.

38. Miller, *The Disappearance of God*, p. 3.

39. Ibid., p. 6.

40. Ibid., p. 7.

41. *L* I, 161–62.

42. Miller, *The Disappeaarnce of God*, p. 1.

43. *JP*, p. 127.

44. As Philip Endean, S.J., says, "The bold, fertile sacramentalism sits alongside an Ultramontane narrowness of outlook about the salvation of non-Catholics." "The Spirituality of GMH," 126.

45. *SDW*, pp. 198–99.

46. *L* I, 83.

Bibliography

Abbott, C. C., ed. *The Correspondence of Gerard Manley Hopkins and Richard Watson Dixon*. Oxford, 1935. (*L* II)

———. *Further Letters of Gerard Manley Hopkins*. Oxford, 1938. (*L* III)

———. *The Letters of Gerard Manley Hopkins and Robert Bridges*. Oxford, 1935. (*L* I)

Baker, James V. *The Sacred River: Coleridge's Theory of the Imagination*. Louisiana State, 1957.

Ball, Patricia M. *The Science of Aspects*. London, 1971.

Barth, J. Robert, S.J. *Coleridge and Christian Doctrine*. Cambridge, Mass., 1969.

———. *The Symbolic Imagination: Coleridge and the Romantic Tradition*. Princeton, 1977.

Bate, Walter Jackson, ed. *Criticism: The Major Texts*. New York, 1952.

Bergonzi, Bernard. *Gerard Manley Hopkins*. New York, 1977.

Bottrall, Margaret, ed. *Gerard Manley Hopkins: Poems, A Casebook*. London, 1975.

Bridges, Robert, ed. *The Poems of Gerard Manley Hopkins* (first edition). Oxford, 1918.

Christ, Carol T. *The Finer Optic*. New Haven, Conn., 1974.

Cotter, James Finn. *Inscape*. Pittsburgh, Pa., 1972.

137

Coulson, John. *Newman and the Common Tradition.* Oxford, 1970.

Davie, Donald. *Purity of Diction in English Verse.* London, 1967.

Devlin, Christopher J., S.J. *The Psychology of Duns Scotus.* Oxford, 1950.

————, ed. *The Sermons and Devotional Writings of Gerard Manley Hopkins.* Oxford, 1959. (*SDW*)

Dunne, Tom. *Gerard Manley Hopkins: A Comprehensive Bibliography.* London, 1976.

Endean, Philip, S.J. "The Spirituality of GMH," *The Hopkins Quarterly,* VIII, 3 (Fall 1981), 107–29.

Freeman, Rosemary. *English Emblem Books.* London, 1948.

Gardner, W. H. *Gerard Manley Hopkins: A Study of Poetic Idiosyncrasy in Relation to Poetic Tradition.* 2 vols. London, 1949.

————, ed. *The Complete Poems of Gerard Manley Hopkins* (fourth edition). Oxford, 1967.

Hartman, Geoffrey. *The Unmediated Vision.* New Haven, Conn., 1954.

House, Humphry. *All in Due Time: The Collected Essays and Broadcast Talks.* London, 1955.

————, and Graham Storey, eds. *The Journals and Papers of Gerard Manley Hopkins.* Oxford, 1959. (*JP*)

Kapitulka, Krystyna. *Structural Principles of Gerard Manley Hopkins' Poetry.* Warsaw, 1976.

Kenyon Critics. *Gerard Manley Hopkins.* London, 1949.

Kermode, Frank, ed. *The Metaphysical Poets.* New York, 1969.

Kitchen, Paddy. *Gerard Manley Hopkins.* New York, 1979.

Lahey, Gerard F., S.J. *Gerard Manley Hopkins.* London, 1930.

Leavis, F. R. *New Bearings in English Poetry.* London, 1932.

Leggio, James. "The Science of a Sacrament," *The Hopkins Quarterly,* IV, 2 (Summer 1977).

Mariani, Paul. *A Commentary on the Complete Poems of Gerard Manley Hopkins.* Ithaca, N.Y., 1970.

Marks, Emerson R. *Coleridge and the Language of Verse.* Princeton, N.J., 1981.

Martz, Louis L. *The Poetry of Meditation.* New Haven, Conn., 1954.

McChesney, Donald. *A Hopkins Commentary*. London, 1968.
Miller, J. Hillis. *The Disappearance of God*. Cambridge, Mass., 1975.
———. *The Linguistic Moment*. Princeton, N.J., 1985.
Milroy, James. *The Language of Gerard Manley Hopkins*. London, 1978.
Norman, E. R. *Anti-Catholicism in Victorian England*. New York, 1968.
Pater, Walter. *The Renaissance* (first edition, 1873). New York, 1959.
Phare, E. E. *The Poetry of Gerard Manley Hopkins*. Cambridge, 1933.
Pick, John. *Gerard Manley Hopkins: Priest and Poet*. London, 1942.
Praz, Mario. *Studies in Seventeenth-Century Imagery*. London, 1939.
Puhl, Louis J., S.J. *The Spiritual Exercises of St. Ignatius*. Chicago, 1951.
Rader, Louis. "Romantic Structure and Theme in Hopkins' Poetry," The Hopkins Quarterly, I, 2 (July 1974).
Raine, Kathleen. "Hopkins—Nature and Supernature," Third Annual Lecture (1972), The Hopkins Society.
Read, Herbert. *English Prose Style*. New York, 1952.
Ritz, Jean-Georges. *Le Poète Gerard Manley Hopkins, S.J.* Paris, 1963.
———. *Robert Bridges and Gerard Manley Hopkins, A Literary Friendship*. London, 1960.
Ross, Malcolm M. *Poetry and Dogma*. Rutgers, 1954.
Sambrook, James, ed. *Pre-Raphaelitism*. Chicago, 1974.
Segel, Harold B. *The Baroque Poem*. New York, 1974.
Sprinker, Michael. *"A Counterpoint of Dissonance": The Aesthetics and Poetry of Gerard Manley Hopkins*. Baltimore, Md., 1980.
Stanford, Donald E., ed. *The Selected Letters of Robert Bridges*. 2 vols. London, 1983, 1984.
Tennyson, G. B. *Victorian Devotional Poetry: The Tractarian Mode*. Cambridge, Mass., 1981.
Wain, John. "An Idiom of Desperation," Chatterton Lecture on

an English Poet, British Academy Pamphlet, Proceedings of the British Academy, XLV, 1959.

Ward, Bernadette. "Poet and Priest in the Terrible Sonnets: Gerard Manley Hopkins." Senior Honors Thesis, HU 1981.

Warren, Austin. *Richard Crashaw: A Study in Baroque Sensibility.* Baton Rouge, La., 1939.

Wellek, René. *Concepts of Criticism.* New Haven, Conn., 1963.

Weyand, Norman, S.J. *Immortal Diamond.* London, 1941.

Wimsatt, W. K. *The Verbal Icon.* Lexington, 1954.

Wölfflin, Heinrich. *Renaissance and Baroque,* translated by Kathrin Simon. Ithaca, N.Y., 1966.

Index